Country Living

Breads & Muffins

Breads & Muffins

THE EDITORS OF
COUNTRY LIVING MAGAZINE

Foreword by Rachel Newman

Country Living

HEARST BOOKS · NEW YO

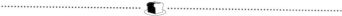

Photography Credits
Pages 17, 53, Richard Jeffery; Pages 18, 71, 72, Charles Gold;
Page 35, John Uher; Page 36, Dennis M. Gottlieb; Page 54, Steve Lovi

•

Acknowledgments appear on page 88.

•

Library of Congress Cataloging-in-Publication Data
Country Living
Country living, country baker. Breads & muffins :
foreword by Rachel Newman. — 1st ed.
p. cm.
Includes index.
ISBN 0-688-12544-1 (alk. paper)
1. Bread. 2. Muffins. I. Country living (New York, N.Y.)
II. Title. III. Title: Breads & muffins. IV. Title: Breads and muffins.
V. Title: Country baker.
TX769.C67   1993
641.8'15—dc20   92-33224
                              •   CIP

Printed in Singapore
First Edition
2 3 4 5 6 7 8 9 10

•

Country Living Staff
Rachel Newman, *Editor-in-Chief*
Lucy Wing, *Contributing Food Editor*
Joanne Lamb Hayes, *Food Editor*
Elaine Van Dyne, *Associate Food Editor*

Produced by Smallwood and Stewart, Inc., New York City

Edited by Judith Blahnik
Designed by Tom Starace
Cover designed by Lynn Pieroni Fowler

Contents

ETHNIC BREADS..II
From our collection of Old World-inspired breads,
here are the crusty loaves reminiscent of breads that
have been made in Ireland, Italy, France, and
Eastern Europe for hundreds of years.

*Irish Freckle Bread, Focaccia, Sourdough Bread, Dark Rye
Bread, Olive Bread, Fougassette, Italian Loaf Rustica,
Kalach*

COUNTRY & WHOLE GRAIN LOAVES 26
This is our collection of the breads that have been
real American favorites for generations.

*Braided Country Loaf, Salt Risin' Bread, Sally Lunn,
Liberty Bread, Hearth Loaf, Ruthie's Perfect Wheat Bread,
Corn Light Bread, Vermont Oatmeal Bread, Whole-Wheat
Toasting Bread, Casserole Health Bread, Whole-Wheat
Bread, Whole-Wheat Rolls, or Cottage Loaf*

DINNER & SANDWICH ROLLS 40
From the popular soft dinner roll to spicy
sandwich and cocktail rolls, these recipes
satisfy cravings for "just a little" bread.

*Buttery Fantan Rolls, Coffee Rye Rolls, Clover Leaf Potato
Rolls, Pepper Rolls, Zucchini Dinner Rolls, Whole-Grain
Crescent Rolls*

SAVORY BREADS..48
If it's spicy, filled with herbs, touched with the tang of cheese or garlic, or sprinkled with oil and salt, the loaf is included in this batch of zesty breads.

Peppered Squash Bread, Garlic Braid, Herbed Potato-Cheese Bread, Country Dill Bread, Herb Garden Bread, Rye and Indian Bread, Garlic-Onion Bread, Cheesy Wheat Bread, Assorted Breadsticks With Herb Butter, Garlic Bread

SWEET LOAVES & QUICK BREADS.............................62
Wonderful for breakfast or tea, these are the fruity pull-apart breads and citrus loaves that are perfect served warm, fresh from the oven.

Finnish Coffee Bread, Apple Pull-Apart Bread, Pear-Butter Bread, The Della Robbia Wreath, Lemon Sesame Loaf

SWEET & SAVORY MUFFINS 73
Better by the dozen, we include twelve muffins that vary from the fancy raspberry to the reliable corn muffin. Try them all.

Pleasant Hill Squash Muffins, Apple Muffins, Carrot-Honey-Date Muffins, Cheddar-Apple Muffins, Sweet Jammies, Raspberry Streusel Muffins, Pear-Hazelnut Muffins, Bostonian Blueberry Muffins, Crunchy Oat and Cranberry Muffins, Apple Muffins With Corn Bran, Banana-Date-Nut Muffins, Corn Muffins

Foreword

L ike no other food, bread represents the pleasures of a simpler time. The sight of bread dough slowly rising on the kitchen counter is even more appealing today because of the hectic world we live in. It is the supreme symbol of hearth and home.

I remember as a child stealing away to some quiet spot to devour the warm slices of bread smothered in jam that my mother had just baked. Traveling through Europe after college I feasted for pennies on the fresh baguettes and loaves of the local bakers. Today I enjoy bread more than ever, having discovered the savory possibilities and rewards of baking my own. Few activities satisfy me more than taking the time to indulge in the ritual of preparing bread.

While the basics of bread preparation remain virtually unchanged, the variations seem almost limitless. The daily tide of *Country Living* staff members flocking from the bakery near my office is evidence enough. They return loaded with all kinds of goods, from hearty dark breads of old to new-age muffins chock full of berries. Their booty is inevitably devoured by noon. The great brick ovens of old may be vanishing, but the joys of baking and eating bread remain as strong as ever.

Rachel Newman
Editor-in-Chief

Introduction

....

WHAT HYMNS ARE SUNG,

WHAT PRAISES SAID,

FOR HOMEMADE MIRACLES OF BREAD?

Louis Untermeyer

If there is one enduring symbol of home, comfort, and security, it is the golden loaf of just-baked bread cooling in the kitchen. Here is a collection of recipes that we hope will tempt you away from airy store-bought loaves and bring you back to the fine-textured homemade breads that have provided comfort and sustenance in American households for three hundred years. We have gathered recipes that reflect a diverse culinary culture — dark rye bread and sourdough from Eastern Europe, savory Mediterranean olive and herb loaves, focaccia from Italy, French fougassette, traditional country whole-wheat and Vermont oatmeal breads, frontier skillet loaves, festive sweet breads, and all-American muffins.

About The Ingredients

Our bread and muffin recipes require all-purpose wheat flour, rye and whole-wheat flours, cornmeal, and occasionally bread flour. Either dark or light rye flours are fine when rye is called for. The dark (sometimes called pumpernickel flour) is coarser in texture and is better for heartier breads. Stone-ground unbleached flour is a fine substitute for all-purpose flour if you care to use it. We use fresh double-acting baking powder in our muffins. Check the date on the can to make sure yours is fresh. If there's any doubt, stir 1 teaspoonful into ½ cup hot water. A bubbling reaction means that the baking powder is fresh.

We use active dry yeast because it is readily available and reliable. Check the date printed on the packet to make sure the yeast is still potent. If you have any doubt, stir ½ teaspoon yeast and ¼ teaspoon sugar into ¼ cup warm (105°F to 115°F) water. If there is a bubbling reaction after 5 or 10 minutes, the yeast is alive. Some recipes use rapid-rising yeast, which works in half the time. To substitute active dry yeast in a recipe that calls for rapid-rising yeast, dissolve the active yeast in lukewarm liquid first and double the dough's rising time.

Butter is lightly salted and always in the stick, as is margarine if you choose to use it. Don't substitute tub or whipped butter, or liquid or tub margarine. Eggs are always large and should be stored in their cartons in the refrigerator. Do not substitute unless noted in the recipe.

We recommend that you use real, not imitation, vanilla, maple, and almond extracts. The pungent flavor of the authentic extract permeates muffins and some breads like no imitation can. Spices such as cinnamon, allspice, ginger, and cloves should be checked for freshness. If your supply is more than six months old, the spice may deliver disappointing results. Nutmeg is always best when grated from the whole nutmeg. When we call for walnuts, almonds, pecans, or hazelnuts, it's in their natural unblanched state unless otherwise noted.

About The Equipment

Use a 4-quart bowl to mix and ferment the dough. A ceramic or wooden bowl offers the most stable environment, protecting the dough from sudden changes in temperature. Glass is second best. Use a set of metal measuring cups for dry ingredients and glass measuring cups for all liquids. You will need a waist-high work space at least 26-inches square for kneading the dough or a heavy-duty electric mixer. A dough scraper, a handy spatulalike instrument, will help you turn and fold sticky dough. Have a sharp knife for dividing dough and scoring loaves, and a rolling pin for rolling certain doughs.

Use a thermometer to gauge the warmth of the water you add to yeast. Bake the bread on a durable baking sheet or in the size pan or pans we suggest. Pans of medium-weight restaurant-quality aluminum are the all-round best for conduction of heat and a guarantee of even baking. Second-best are ovenproof glass and ceramic. The nonstick metals pans are good choices if you buy the bonded rather than the sprayed-surface pans and also grease them (just to guarantee their non-stick promises).

Loaf pans   5¾ by 3¼ inches
                      9 by 5 by 3 inches
                      8½ by 4½ inches
10-inch tube pan (preferably with a removable bottom)
10-inch decorative tube pan, like a bundt pan or other fluted pan
9-inch springform pan
2½- and 3-inch muffin-pan cups (metal and microwave-safe)
6- and 7-ounce glass or ceramic decorative muffin molds

A wire or wooden cooling rack is a must. Breads actually finish baking as they cool (allow 20 minutes). The rack lets air circulate, preventing the bottom of the bread from becoming soggy.

About The Method

We almost always dissolve the active dry yeast in warm liquid before combining the ingredients for the bread dough. This allows the yeast to come alive. The temperature is important; no less than 105°F but no more than 115°F. High temperatures scald and kill the cells. Use a thermometer until you get the knack of testing the water by feel.

Most of the time, there is a range in the amount of flour called for in bread and the recipe directs you to work in extra flour as you knead the dough. Since absorbency changes from flour to flour, you have to use your sense of touch to know when the dough is no longer sticky and has become smooth and needs no more flour. Measure flour — and all dry ingredients — by dipping the proper metal measuring cup and scooping up and leveling off the excess with a knife or thin metal spatula.

When the recipe says "cool completely on a wire rack" it means to cool to room temperature. To remove a loaf from a pan, run a metal spatula around the edge. Hold the pan with a towel or potholder and turn it upside down. With a firm snap, release the bread into your other hand and place it right-side up on the cooling rack.

Irish Freckle Bread

....

The recipe is from *Bernard Clayton's New Complete Book of Breads.* The freckles are from the addition of sweet raisins.

MAKES 2 LOAVES

1 large (½ pound)
  all-purpose potato, peeled
  and quartered
1½ cups water
5 cups bread or all-purpose
  flour
2 packages active dry yeast
⅓ cup sugar

1 teaspoon salt
2 eggs, lightly beaten
½ cup (1 stick) butter or
  margarine, melted and
  cooled
1 cup dark seedless raisins or
  dried currants

1. In a 1-quart saucepan, cook the potato in the water until the potato is tender, about 20 minutes. With a slotted spoon, remove the potato to a small bowl and mash until broken up. Reserve 1 cup cooking liquid and allow it to cool to 120° to 130°F.

2. In a large bowl, combine 1½ cups flour, the mashed potato, yeast, sugar, and salt. Stir in the cooled cooking liquid until a smooth batter forms. Cover the bowl with a clean, damp cloth and set it in a warm, draft-free place until the batter is puffy, 1 to 1½ hours.

3. Stir down the batter. Add the eggs, butter, and raisins. With a wooden spoon, gradually beat in the remaining 3½ cups flour, ½ cup at a time, to make a soft, manageable dough. Turn onto a lightly floured surface and knead until the dough is smooth and elastic, about 10 minutes. Shape the dough into a ball.

4. Grease two 8½- by 4½-inch loaf pans. Divide the dough in half and shape each half into a ball; let the dough rest 5 minutes. Flatten each ball and shape into an oblong loaf. Place each loaf in a prepared pan. Cover the pans with clean, damp cloths, and set them in a warm, draft-free place, until the dough rises to the rims of the pans, 45 minutes.

5. Heat the oven to 375°F. Bake the loaves 35 minutes, or until they sound hollow when tapped on the top with a fingertip. Remove the loaves from the pans and cool completely on a wire rack.

Focaccia

PHOTOGRAPH ON PAGE 53

This rich-tasting Italian flat bread makes a delicious snack or base for pizza. You can roll it out into different shapes and sizes, making small individual pizzas or large flat loaves that can be cut into squares for serving.

MAKES 4 SERVINGS

1 package active dry yeast
½ teaspoon sugar
1¼ cups warm water
  (105° to 115° F)
3¼ cups bread flour or all-
  purpose flour
¾ teaspoon salt

¼ teaspoon dried thyme
  leaves
½ cup olive oil
4 heads garlic
¼ cup grated Parmesan
  cheese
¼ teaspoon cracked black
  pepper

1. In a large bowl, sprinkle the yeast and sugar over the warm water; let stand until foamy, about 10 minutes.

2. Stir 1½ cups flour into the yeast mixture until smooth. Cover the bowl with a clean, damp cloth and set it in a warm, draft-free place until the dough is puffy and has doubled in size, about 1 hour.

3. In small bowl, combine the salt, thyme, and 1¼ cups of flour. Stir the flour mixture into the yeast mixture along with 3 tablespoons olive oil to form a soft dough. Turn the dough onto a lightly floured surface and knead, working in remaining flour if necessary until the dough is smooth and elastic, about 10 minutes. (The dough will be sticky.)

4. Shape the dough into a ball and place it in a large, lightly oiled bowl, turning once to bring the oiled side up. Cover the bowl loosely with a clean, damp cloth and set it in a warm, draft-free place until the dough has doubled in size, 35 to 40 minutes.

5. Meanwhile, arrange the oven racks so that one is at the bottom position and one is center. Heat the oven to 350°F. Separate the garlic bulbs into cloves. On a rimmed baking sheet, toss the unpeeled cloves with 1 tablespoon oil; spread out on the baking sheet. Bake on the center rack of the oven 20 to 30 minutes, or until the garlic is soft. Cool slightly; remove the skins and split the cloves in half.

6. Lightly grease 2 large baking sheets and sprinkle them with corn-meal. Punch down the dough and divide it in half. Using a floured rolling pin, roll each half out on a prepared baking sheet into 14- to 16-inch rounds. Brush the rounds with the remaining oil. Top each round with half the garlic cloves, Parmesan cheese, and black pepper. Press the garlic cloves into the dough.

7. Increase the oven temperature to 475°F. Bake the focaccia, one baking sheet on each rack, 15 minutes. Rotate the baking sheets, moving the one on the bottom rack to the top and the one on the top rack to the bottom. Bake the focaccia 10 minutes longer, or until golden brown. Serve hot from the oven; break or cut into wedges at the table.

Y E A S T   A L I V E !

Yeast is a living plant cell; billions of the wild microscopic cells are in the air around us, everywhere. The thin white film we see on a grape is a gathering of yeast, which is feeding on the sugar in the fruit. Sugar is the main diet of yeast, and when it finds enough to consume in a warm environment, it feeds and reproduces at an amazing rate, sometimes doubling the number of cells in 30 minutes.

Active dry yeast is moist yeast (like that on the grape) that has been produced commercially, then dried. In an airtight, cool environment, the dried yeast remains asleep. But when awakened with oxygen and warm water and fed with fresh flour and sugar, it begins to feed ravenously and reproduce. This "feeding frenzy" causes fermentation, which produces two elements that are very good for bread: carbon dioxide gas, which makes the dough rise and gives the inner crumb an airy, dense texture; and alcohol, which permeates and flavors the dough.

Most bread dough goes through at least two hours of fermentation. It should be kept warm (about 80°F) in a draft-free place so the yeast has a stable and helpful environment in which to grow. If the dough is too warm, the yeast will be accelerated, producing too much gas too quickly. Your bread will be fluffy, gassy, and yeasty-tasting. If the dough is too cold, the yeast will be sluggish and the bread won't rise well at all.

Sourdough Bread

PHOTOGRAPH ON PAGE 17

The name comes from the light sour tang the "starter" produces when added to the dough. The starter is simply a little bit of dough that has been fermenting longer than twenty four hours. When it is mixed into your bread dough, it brings moisture and unusual flavor to the loaf.

MAKES 1 LARGE OR 2 SMALL LOAVES

Starter:
1 package active dry yeast
1 tablespoon sugar
1½ cups warm water
  (105° to 115° F)
1½ cups all-purpose flour

Bread:
1 package active dry yeast
1 tablespoon sugar

1¾ cups warm water
  (105° to 115° F)
1 cup starter
7 to 7½ cups all-purpose
  flour
1½ teaspoons salt
¼ teaspoon baking soda

1. Prepare the Starter: In a medium-size bowl, sprinkle the yeast and sugar over the warm water and let the mixture stand until foamy, 5 minutes. Beat in the flour until smooth. Cover the bowl with a clean, damp cloth and set it in a draft-free place at room temperature overnight. Refrigerate the starter at least 3 more days, or until ready to use. Stir once a day. Replace each cup of starter used with ½ cup flour, 1 teaspoon sugar, and ½ cup warm water.

2. Prepare the Bread: In a large bowl, sprinkle the yeast and sugar over the warm water and let the mixture stand until foamy, 5 minutes.

3. Stir the starter, 6½ cups flour, salt, and baking soda into the yeast mixture to make a soft manageable dough. Knead the dough in the bowl until it forms a ball. Turn onto a lightly floured surface and knead, working in as much of the remaining 1 cup flour as necessary, until the dough is smooth and elastic, about 10 minutes.

4. Shape the dough into a ball and place the dough in a large, lightly oiled bowl, turning once to bring the oiled side up. Cover the bowl with a clean, damp cloth, and set it in a warm, draft-free place, until the dough has doubled in size, 45 to 50 minutes.

5. Lightly grease 1 or 2 baking sheets. Punch down the dough and shape into 1 or 2 round or long loaves. Place the loaves on the prepared baking sheets. Cover with a clean, damp cloth, and place in a warm, draft-free place, until the loaves have doubled in size, 45 to 50 minutes.

6. Heat the oven to 400°F. With a sharp knife, score the loaves by cutting 2 or 3 slits ½-inch deep across the top of each loaf. Bake the loaves 25 to 30 minutes, or until they are golden brown and sound hollow when tapped on the top with a fingertip. Remove the loaves from the baking sheets and cool completely on wire racks.

T H E   S C O R E   A N D   T H E   C R U S T

Making scores about ½ inch deep into the loaf at a slight angle allows steam heat to escape while the loaf bakes, and as the expanding bread pushes through the scores, the visual character of your bread takes shape. In France there are rules about scoring — baguettes, for example, must have seven diagonal cuts. Here there are no rules, so you can experiment and develop your own style. A gridlike score of two cuts in one direction and two cuts crossing them is handsome for rustic loaves, while a single-slash, half-moon style or a starburst over the top of the same loaf will produce a whole different look.

For a crispy crust on a robust bread, start the bread in an oven filled with steam so that steam covers the loaf with moisture during the first minutes of baking. As baking continues, the moisture evaporates, creating a crisp crust. There are two methods for accomplishing this. One is to place a shallow pan filled with hot water on the bottom of a preheated oven 5 to 10 minutes before putting the bread in the oven. Another, more hands-on method is to place the breads in a preheated oven and spray the walls of the oven with cold water from a spritzer bottle (don't hit the oven light). Close the door quickly to trap the steam. Do this three times during the first 5 minutes of baking.

Dark Rye Bread

··········

R ye flour produces an aromatic and flavorful loaf, and for a rustic old-world look, use dark, stone-ground rye flour (sometimes called pumpernickel flour). This bread makes a terrific sandwich. Try it with sprouts and a tangy soft cheese.

MAKES 2 LOAVES

2 packages active dry yeast
1½ cups warm water
* (105° to 115° F)*
½ cup dark molasses
2¾ cups rye flour
¼ cup cocoa powder
2 tablespoons caraway seeds

2 tablespoons vegetable
* shortening*
1 teaspoon salt
2½ to 3 cups all-purpose flour
2 to 3 tablespoons yellow
* cornmeal*

1. In a large bowl, sprinkle the yeast over the warm water. Stir in the molasses and let the mixture stand until foamy, about 10 minutes.

2. Stir the rye flour, cocoa, caraway seeds, shortening, and salt into the yeast mixture until smooth. Stir in enough all-purpose flour to make a soft and manageable dough. Turn onto a lightly floured surface and knead, working in remaining flour if necessary, until the dough is smooth and elastic, about 10 minutes.

3. Shape the dough into a ball and place in a large, lightly oiled bowl, turning once to bring the oiled side up. Cover the bowl with a clean, damp cloth and set it in a warm, draft-free place until the dough has doubled in size, about 1 hour. Punch down the dough. Cover the bowl again, and set it in a warm, draft-free place until the dough has doubled in size, about 20 minutes.

4. Grease a baking sheet and sprinkle it with cornmeal. Punch down the dough and divide it in half. Shape each half into an oval loaf. Place the loaves at opposite ends of the baking sheet. Cover the baking sheet with a clean damp cloth and set it in a warm, draft-free place until the loaves have doubled in size, about 40 minutes.

5. Heat the oven to 375°F. Score the loaves and bake 30 to 35 minutes, or until they sound hollow when tapped on the top with a fingertip. Remove the loaves from the baking sheet and cool completely on wire racks.

Sourdough Bread, page 14

Herbed Potato-Cheese Bread, page 52

Olive Bread

....

Both the French and the Italians have long traditions of making breads with the rich addition of native-grown olives. Be sure to use Mediterranean oil-cured olives for the best flavor and texture. Baking with steam ensures a crisp crust with a country crackle.

MAKES 1 LOAF

3 to 3½ cups bread flour	*⅓ cup pitted, chopped, oil-*
1 package active dry yeast	*cured ripe olives*
2 tablespoons sugar	*2 tablespoons olive oil*
1 cup warm water	*1 teaspoon salt*
(105° to 115° F)	*Boiling water*
	Warm water

1. In a large bowl, combine ½ cup flour, the yeast, and sugar. Stir in the water; let the mixture stand until foamy, about 10 minutes. Stir 2 cups flour, the olives, oil, and salt into the yeast mixture to make a soft manageable dough. Turn onto a lightly floured surface and knead, working in as much of the remaining flour as necessary, until the dough is smooth and elastic, about 10 minutes.

2. Shape the dough into a ball and place in a large, lightly oiled bowl, turning once to bring the oiled side up. Cover the bowl with a clean, damp cloth, and set it in a warm, draft-free place until the dough has doubled in size, about 1 hour.

3. Lightly grease a baking sheet. Punch down the dough and roll it out into a 12- by 8-inch oval. Starting from the long side, roll the dough over 2 inches; pinch to make a tight seam. Continue rolling the dough in 2-inch increments, pinching the seam with each turn, to form a 12-inch-long roll. Pinch the final seam and ends tightly. Gently pull and taper the ends of the rolled dough. Place the loaf on the prepared baking sheet. Cover the sheet with a clean, damp cloth, and set it in a warm, draft-free place, until the loaf has doubled in size, about 40 minutes.

4. Heat the oven to 400°F. Place a deep roasting pan on the bottom rack of the oven. Pour 1 inch boiling water into the pan to create steam for baking the bread. Brush the top of the bread with warm water. Score the loaf and bake 35 to 40 minutes, or until it is lightly golden. Remove the loaf from the baking sheet and cool completely on a wire rack.

Fougassette

....

Traditional French *fougass* is a large, flat, irregularly shaped bread. It's made to tear apart easily and eat with soups or mop up dressings and sauces. Our *fougassette* is a mini-version. For variation, sprinkle with coarse salt or sesame seeds just before baking.

MAKES 4 SMALL BREADS

6 slices bacon, chopped	2½ to 3 cups all-purpose
1 package active dry yeast	flour
¾ cup warm water	2 tablespoons olive oil
(105° to 115° F)	1 teaspoon salt
1 tablespoon sugar	1 egg
	2 tablespoons water

1. In a large skillet, cook the bacon over medium heat until crisp. Remove the bacon from the skillet; drain and crumble. Reserve the bacon and 3 tablespoons drippings.

2. In a large bowl, sprinkle the yeast over the water. Stir in the sugar and let the mixture stand until foamy, about 10 minutes.

3. Stir 1½ cups flour, the oil, salt, and the reserved bacon and drippings into the yeast mixture until smooth, about 3 minutes. Stir in 1 cup flour to make a soft manageable dough. Turn onto a lightly floured surface and lightly knead, working in as much of the remaining ½ cup flour as necessary to prevent sticking, 2 minutes.

4. Shape the dough into a ball and place in a large, lightly oiled bowl, turning once to bring the oiled side up. Cover the bowl with a clean, damp cloth, and set it in a warm, draft-free place until the dough has doubled in size, about 1 hour.

5. Grease 2 baking sheets. Punch down the dough and divide it into 4 pieces. Roll one piece into an 8- by 6-inch rectangle, making the edges slightly thicker than the center. With a sharp knife, starting 1¼ inches from the edge, cut 3 rows of lengthwise diagonal slits, about 1 inch long and 1 inch apart. Place the dough on one prepared baking sheet; with your fingers, open the slits to create elongated holes in the dough. Repeat the process with the remaining 3 pieces of dough. Cover the baking sheets with clean, damp cloths, and set them in a warm, draft-free place, until the breads have doubled in size, 30 minutes.

6. Heat the oven to 400°F. In a small bowl, lightly beat the egg and 2 tablespoons water. Brush the dough with the egg mixture, widening the holes if necessary. Bake the loaves 12 to 15 minutes, or until lightly browned and barely crisp. Cool the breads slightly on wire racks.

T H E   N E E D   F O R   K N E A D I N G

Kneading is a process that tends to intimidate beginners. Granted, the dough is alive, but it is a durable substance and very forgiving. Accomplished bakers love to work the dough with their hands; they know that unless it is well kneaded, it will not rise well and will not produce the texture we've come to expect in fine breads.

The hands-on kneading develops the gluten in the dough. Gluten is protein found in most flours. As you push, pummel, and wrestle the dough, the gluten becomes a web of musclelike strings. This web traps the carbon dioxide gas produced during fermentation, which then makes the dough rise. Without a well-kneaded dough, there would be no lofty, flavorful bread with light crumb.

Tips for beginners: Begin with a lumpy mass of soft dough in a bowl. Turn it onto a lightly floured surface, about 26 inches square, waist-high, and sturdy — a countertop is fine. If the dough is sticky, lift it with a dough scraper or metal spatula and fold it in half. Sprinkle it with a little extra flour. Push down with the heel of your hand, pushing at an angle away from your body and using your body weight to lean forward. As you pull back, pull the dough back with your other hand, give it a quarter turn, and fold it again. Repeat the process of push forward, pull back, turn, and fold, and push. Sprinkle with more flour as you knead until any moist stickiness disappears. After 5 minutes you will notice elasticity and life in the dough. Continue kneading until the dough is smooth and elastic. It may take 10 minutes. Test it by pressing a finger into it and making an indentation. If the dough springs back into place when you remove your finger, it is ready to rise.

Italian Loaf Rustica

....

L ayered with spicy sausage, peppers, onions, and cheese, this Pillsbury Bake-Off® winner is a no-knead batter bread that's almost a meal in itself. Serve it with a salad for a light lunch or supper.

MAKES 1 LOAF

1 pound sweet Italian sausage	1½ cups very warm water (120° to 130° F)
½ cup chopped onion	2 teaspoons butter or margarine, softened
2 to 4 cloves garlic, finely chopped	½ pound mozzarella cheese, cut into cubes
1½ cups all-purpose flour	1 7-ounce jar roasted red peppers, drained and chopped
½ cup whole-wheat flour	
½ cup yellow cornmeal	
1 tablespoon sugar	1 egg, beaten
½ teaspoon salt	2 to 3 teaspoons sesame seeds
1 package rapid-rising dry yeast	

1. Into a large skillet, crumble the sausage (if the sausage comes in a casing, remove and discard the casing). Add the onion and garlic; saute over medium-high heat, until the sausage is browned, about 6 to 8 minutes. Drain off the fat; set the sausage mixture aside.

2. In a large bowl, combine ½ cup all-purpose flour, the whole-wheat flour, cornmeal, sugar, salt, and yeast. Stir the water, butter and the remaining all-purpose flour into the flour mixture to make a soft, manageable dough. Cover the bowl with a clean, damp cloth, and let the dough rest in a warm draft-free place 10 minutes.

3. Grease a 9- or 10-inch springform pan. Stir down the dough. With greased fingers, press about two thirds of the dough into the bottom of the prepared pan. Add the cheese and peppers to the sausage mixture and spoon the mixture into the center of the dough. Spread the filling towards the edge of the pan, leaving a ½-inch border of dough. Drop the remaining dough, by tablespoonfuls, over the filling. With the back of a spoon, spread the dough to cover the filling (the top will be rough). Cover the pan with a clean, damp cloth, and set it in a warm, draft-free place until the dough has doubled in size, 20 to 30 minutes.

4. Heat the oven to 400°F. Brush the top of the dough with the egg and sprinkle with the sesame seeds. Bake the loaf 25 to 30 minutes, or until it is golden brown and pulls away from the side of the pan. Cool the bread in the pan 5 minutes. With a sharp knife loosen the edge of the bread in the pan; remove the side of the pan. Cut the bread into wedges and serve warm. Refrigerate any remaining bread.

PROBLEMS? WHAT HAPPENED?

The dough didn't rise: The yeast may have been inactive. If you have any doubt about the potency of your yeast, you can find out if it is alive by sprinkling ¼ teaspoon over ¼ cup warm water with 1 teaspoon sugar dissolved in it. If bubbles or foam appear within 5 or 10 minutes, the yeast is potent.

The added water or liquid may have been too hot. High heat kills the yeast. DON'T ADD LIQUID HIGHER IN TEMPERATURE THAN 140°F.

The flour you're using may not have enough protein to make a dough strong enough to trap and hold in the carbon dioxide produced during fermentation. Check to make sure you are using a good quality flour with a protein content of at least 11 percent.

The baked loaf is too small: If the yeast remains healthy, moderately active, and strong during fermentation, it will have one last burst of life when you put the loaf in the sudden high heat of the oven. This burst causes the loaf to puff up into its lovely high shape. If the loaf is too small, you may have added too much salt, which retards the activity of the yeast.

The dough may have fermented in too cool a place, making the yeast too sluggish to respond to the oven temperature.

Your oven temperature may have been too high, which would char the loaf before it had time to spring up to a nice loft.

Kalach (Egg Bread)

....

This Ukrainian bread is traditionally served on Christmas Eve. It's baked in three rings to represent the Trinity. When served, the three rings are stacked and a candle is placed in the middle.

MAKES ONE 3-RING LOAF

9 to 10 cups all-purpose
  flour
½ cup sugar
3 packages rapid-rising dry
  yeast
1 teaspoon salt

6 tablespoons butter or
  margarine, softened
4 eggs
6 egg yolks
2 cups very warm water
  (120° to 130° F)
1 teaspoon cold water

1. In a very large bowl, combine 9 cups flour, the sugar, yeast, salt, and butter. In a medium-size bowl, combine the eggs, 4 egg yolks, and the water. Stir the egg mixture into the flour mixture to make a soft, manageable dough. Turn onto a lightly floured surface and knead, working in as much of the remaining 1 cup flour as necessary, until the dough is smooth and elastic, about 10 minutes.

2. Shape the dough into a ball and place in a large, lightly oiled bowl, turning once to bring the oiled side up. Cover the bowl with a clean, damp cloth and set it in a warm, draft-free place until the dough has doubled in size, 35 to 40 minutes.

3. Grease 2 large baking sheets. Punch down the dough and divide it in half; set one dough half aside. Divide the other half into 3 pieces. Roll each piece into a 28-inch rope. Braid the ropes and shape into a ring, pinching the ends of the ropes together. Place the loaf on one prepared baking sheet.

4. Divide the other dough half into 2 pieces, one piece twice as large as the other. Divide the larger piece into thirds. Roll each third into a 20-inch rope. Braid the ropes and shape into a ring, pinching the ends together. Place the loaf on the other prepared baking sheet. Repeat the process with the remaining piece of dough, rolling each third into 14-inch ropes, braiding, and shaping into a small ring. Place the loaf on the baking sheet with the medium-size loaf. Cover the loaves with

clean, damp cloths, and set the baking sheets in a warm, draft-free place until the loaves have doubled in size, 20 minutes.

5. Heat the oven to 350°F. In a small bowl, combine the remaining 2 egg yolks and the cold water. Brush the loaves with some of the egg yolk mixture and bake 25 minutes. Brush the loaves with the remaining egg yolk mixture; bake 5 to 10 minutes longer, or until golden brown. Cool the loaves on wire racks. To serve, stack the loaves, starting with the largest loaf on the bottom and ending with the smallest loaf on the top. Insert a candle through the center of the loaves, if desired.

PROBLEMS? WHAT HAPPENED?

The loaf has no golden color: The natural sugar in the flour and the added sugar in the recipe caramelize during baking, the reason for the golden color of an eye-catching loaf. If you forgot to add sugar to the dough, or if the fermentation temperature was too high, the yeast cells would eat all the sugar, leaving none to caramelize. An oven temperature that's too low might also be the reason.

The loaf looks great but tastes like yeast: The rising time was too long at too high a temperature, resulting in yeast that produced a lot of gas but not enough alcohol to flavor the dough, or you may have added too much yeast.

The pan loaf has pale sides and bottom: Depending on the baking pan, the bread will brown well or not very much on the sides. Unmold the bread and bake it another 10 minutes.

There are big holes in the interior crumb: Too much yeast produces too much gas. Punching the dough down between risings was not vigorous enough. Hit the dough in the center with your fist. You will hear the gas escape. This deflates the dough, getting rid of the old gas and invigorating the yeast for a second rising.

Braided Country Loaf

....

Of all the breads in a country bakery window, this is probably the first one to catch your eye. A golden braided ring, it is a show-piece. Place it in the center of the table.

MAKES 1 LOAF

6 to 6½ cups all-purpose flour	1¾ cups very warm water
2 packages rapid-rising dry yeast	(120° to 130° F)
2 tablespoons sugar	2 tablespoons butter or
1½ teaspoons salt	margarine, softened
	2 eggs

1. In a large bowl, combine 5 cups flour, the yeast, sugar, and salt. Stir the water, butter, and eggs into the flour mixture to make a soft, manageable dough. Add 1 cup flour and knead the dough in the bowl, working in the flour, until the dough is smooth.

2. Turn the dough onto a lightly floured surface and knead, working in as much of the remaining flour as necessary, until the dough is smooth and elastic, about 10 minutes. Shape the dough into a ball; cover with a clean, damp cloth and let it rest 20 minutes.

3. Lightly grease a baking sheet. Divide the dough into 4 pieces. Set aside one piece. Pinch off a 1-inch ball of dough from each of the 3 remaining pieces. Knead the balls together and set aside. Shape each of the 3 pieces into a 24-inch rope. Loosely braid the ropes and shape into a ring on the prepared baking sheet, pinching the ends together to seal the ring. Flatten the reserved ball of dough in the center of the ring.

4. Divide the reserved piece of dough into 3 pieces and roll each piece into a 10-inch rope. Loosely braid the ropes and shape into a ring, pinching the ends together to seal the ring. Place the ring on top of the larger ring, covering the ball of dough in the center. Cover the baking sheet with a clean, damp cloth and set it in a warm, draft-free place, until the loaf has doubled in size, about 35 to 40 minutes.

5. Heat the oven to 350°F. Bake the ring 35 to 40 minutes, or until it sounds hollow when tapped on the top with a fingertip. Cool the ring completely on a wire rack.

Salt Risin' Bread

Bakers in the 19th Century could make breads rise without yeast — if they added a fermenting mixture of salt, sugar, and potato to the dough. The concoction not only leavened the bread but created great flavor as well. We add yeast just to guarantee good results.

MAKES TWO 8-INCH LOAVES OR 1 DOUBLE LOAF

1 medium potato, peeled and finely chopped	*1 package active dry yeast*
	1 cup milk
1½ cups boiling water	*5½ to 6 cups all-purpose flour*
3 tablespoons cornmeal	*¼ teaspoon baking soda*
2 teaspoons sugar	*1 egg white (optional)*
1 teaspoon salt	*Water (optional)*

1. In a medium-size bowl, combine the potato, boiling water, cornmeal, sugar, and salt. Cover and let stand at room temperature overnight.

2. Strain the potato mixture, reserving 1 cup of the liquid. In a small bowl sprinkle the yeast over the liquid; let stand until dissolved. In a small saucepan, heat the milk over medium heat until bubbles form around the side of the pan. Remove from the heat; cool to room temperature, 70° to 75°F.

3. In a large bowl, combine 5 cups flour, the baking soda, and yeast mixture. Stir in the cooled milk to make a soft, manageable dough. Turn onto a lightly floured surface and knead, working in as much of the remaining flour as necessary, until the dough is smooth and elastic, about 10 minutes. Shape the dough into a ball; cover with a clean, damp cloth and let it rest 5 minutes.

4. Grease and flour two 8½- by 4½-inch loaf pans or an 11- by 4.5-inch pâté mold. Divide the dough in half and shape each half into a ball. Place each ball in a prepared loaf pan. Cover with clean, damp cloths, and set in a warm, draft-free place until the dough has doubled in size, 60 to 70 minutes.

5. Heat the oven to 350°F. If desired, in a small bowl, beat the egg white and a few drops of water and brush over the loaves. Bake the loaves 35 to 40 minutes, or until golden brown and the loaves sound hollow when tapped on the top with a fingertip. Cool the loaves in the pans 5 minutes. Remove the loaves from the pans and cool on wire racks.

Sally Lunn

Legend has it that Sally Lunn was a vendor in Bath, England, during the 18th Century, who did very well selling her butter-rich breads on the street.

MAKES 1 LOAF

1 package active dry yeast
¼ cup warm water
    (105° to 115° F)
¾ cup milk
¼ cup (½ stick) butter or
    margarine

3 cups all-purpose flour
¼ cup sugar
½ teaspoon salt
2 eggs, lightly beaten

1. In a small bowl, sprinkle the yeast over the water; let stand until dissolved, about 5 minutes. In a 1-quart saucepan, heat the milk over medium heat until bubbles form around the side of the pan. Stir in the butter. Remove from the heat; cool to room temperature, 70° to 75°F.

2. In a large bowl, combine the flour, sugar, salt, yeast mixture, cooled milk, and eggs. Beat with a wooden spoon until smooth. Cover the bowl with a clean, damp cloth and set it in a warm, draft-free place until the batter has doubled in size, about 45 minutes.

3. Generously grease and flour a fluted 1½-quart mold, turk's head mold, or 9-inch tube pan. Stir down the batter and pour it into the mold. Cover the mold with a clean, damp cloth and set it in a warm, draft-free place until the dough has doubled in size, about 45 minutes.

4. Heat the oven to 350°F. Bake the bread 40 to 45 minutes, or until it is golden and sounds hollow when tapped on the top with a fingertip. Cool the bread in the mold 5 minutes. Invert the mold, remove the bread and cool completely on a wire rack.

BREAD AT HIGH ALTITUDES

Dough rises rapidly at high altitude. Don't ever use rapid-rising dry yeast. In fact, use half as much yeast as called for. Bake at the regular temperature, but allow double the amount of baking time.

Liberty Bread

....

Bread made with potatoes has long been a favorite of the English, the loaves being tender-moist and producing slices that soak up melting butter in a way no other bread can.

MAKES 1 LOAF

1 large (¾ pound) baking
   potato, peeled and cut
   into eighths
1 cup water
1 package active dry yeast

3 teaspoons butter or
   margarine, melted
2 tablespoons sugar
1 teaspoon salt
3 to 3½ cups all-purpose
   flour

1. In a 1-quart saucepan, cook the potato in the water until tender, about 20 minutes. Remove the potato to a small bowl and mash until well broken up. In a glass measuring cup, reserve the cooking liquid and add enough water to make 1 cup. Cool the liquid to 105° to 115°F.

2. In a large bowl, sprinkle the yeast over the reserved liquid; let stand until dissolved, about 5 minutes. Add the mashed potato, 2 teaspoons butter, the sugar, and salt to the yeast mixture. With an electric mixer on medium speed, beat the potato mixture until smooth.

3. With a wooden spoon, stir 3 cups flour into the potato mixture to make a soft manageable dough. Turn onto a lightly floured surface and knead, working in as much of the remaining flour as necessary, until the dough is smooth and elastic, about 10 minutes.

4. Shape the dough into a ball and place it in a large, lightly oiled bowl, turning once to bring the oiled side up. Cover the bowl with a clean, damp cloth and set it in a warm, draft-free place until the dough has doubled in size, about 30 minutes.

5. Grease a 9- by 5-inch loaf pan. Punch down the dough and shape it into an oblong loaf. Fit the loaf into the prepared pan. Cover with a clean, damp cloth and set it in a warm, draft-free place until the loaf has doubled in size, about 40 minutes.

6. Heat the oven to 350°F. Brush the loaf with the remaining 1 teaspoon butter and bake 55 to 65 minutes, or until golden brown. Cool the loaf in the pan on a wire rack 5 minutes. Remove the bread from the pan and cool completely on the rack.

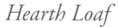

Hearth Loaf

Like a classic peasant loaf of France, this bread bakes up round and golden. Dusting the crust with oat bran flakes, rolled oats, or a mixture of cracked wheat and rye before baking gives it country character and texture.

MAKES 1 LOAF

> 3 packages active dry yeast
> 2¾ cups warm water
>   (105° to 115° F)
> 1½ cups 100% oat bran flakes
> 4 to 4½ cups all-purpose
>   flour
>
> 1½ cups whole-wheat flour
> 1½ cups yellow cornmeal
> 3 tablespoons honey
> 1 teaspoon salt

1. In a large bowl, sprinkle the yeast over the water; let stand until dissolved, about 5 minutes.

2. Stir 1⅓ cups oat bran flakes, 4 cups all-purpose flour, the whole-wheat flour, cornmeal, honey, and salt into the yeast mixture to make a soft, manageable dough. Turn onto a lightly floured surface and knead, working in as much of the remaining ½ cup all-purpose flour as necessary, until the dough is smooth, about 10 minutes.

3. Shape the dough into a ball and place it in a large, lightly oiled bowl, turning once to bring the oiled side up. Cover the bowl with a clean, damp cloth and set it in a warm, draft-free place until the dough has doubled in size, 45 minutes.

4. Lightly grease a baking sheet. Punch down the dough and shape it into a 6-inch-round loaf. Place the loaf on the prepared baking sheet. Cover with a clean, damp cloth and set it in a warm, draft-free place until it has doubled in size, 45 minutes.

5. Heat the oven to 375°F. With a sharp knife, score the loaf by cutting 2 parallel lines across the top of the loaf, about 2½ inches apart and ½ inch deep. Repeat, crisscrossing in the opposite direction. Brush the loaf lightly with water; sprinkle the remaining oat bran flakes on the top.

6. Bake the bread 45 to 50 minutes, or until it is lightly browned and sounds hollow when tapped on the top with a fingertip. Cool the bread completely on a wire rack.

Ruthie's Perfect Wheat Bread

....

W hat's "perfect" is the simple balance of white flour to whole-wheat flour and the hint of sweetness. For a classic look, shape these into free-form shapes, as in Hearth Loaf (page 30). Or bake in pans for perfect toast and sandwich bread.

MAKES 2 LOAVES

1 package active dry yeast
1¾ cups warm water
   (105° to 115° F)
¼ cup firmly packed light-brown
   sugar

3 tablespoons vegetable
   shortening, melted
1 teaspoon salt
3 to 3¼ cups sifted all-purpose
   flour
2 cups whole-wheat flour

1. In a small bowl, sprinkle the yeast over ¼ cup water; let stand until dissolved. In a large bowl, combine the remaining 1½ cups water, the brown sugar, shortening, and salt. Cool to 100°F.

2. With a wooden spoon, stir 1 cup of the all-purpose flour and all the whole-wheat flour into the shortening mixture. Beat well. Stir the yeast mixture into the flour mixture and add enough of the remaining all-purpose flour to make a stiff dough. Turn onto a lightly floured surface and knead, working in as much of the remaining all-purpose flour as necessary, until the dough is smooth and elastic, about 10 minutes.

3. Shape the dough into a ball and place in a large, lightly oiled bowl, turning once to bring the oiled side up. Cover the bowl with a clean, damp cloth and set it in a warm, draft-free place until the dough has doubled in size, about 1½ hours.

4. Heat the oven to 375°F. Grease two 8½- by 4½-inch loaf pans. Punch down the dough and divide it into 2 balls. Cover the dough balls with a clean, damp cloth, and let them rest 10 minutes.

5. Shape the dough into 2 oblong loaves and place each in a prepared pan. Bake the loaves 45 minutes. If the loaves brown too quickly, cover loosely with aluminum foil for the last 20 minutes. Remove the loaves from the pans and cool on wire racks.

Corn Light Bread

....

This no-knead skillet bread is from *Miss Mary's Down-Home Cooking* by Diana Dalsass. The buttermilk gives it a light tang that contrasts with the sweetness of the sugar and the cornmeal.

MAKES ONE SKILLET LOAF

¼ cup (½ stick) butter or
   margarine
2 cups cornmeal
   (preferably white)
1 cup all-purpose flour
¼ cup sugar

1 package active dry yeast
1 teaspoon baking powder
½ teaspoon baking soda
½ teaspoon salt
2½ cups buttermilk, heated
   to 100° F

1. In a heavy cast-iron skillet with an ovenproof handle, melt the butter over low heat. Rotate the skillet slightly to grease the sides.

2. In a large bowl, combine the cornmeal, flour, sugar, yeast, baking powder, baking soda, and salt. Stir the buttermilk into the cornmeal mixture. Spoon the batter into the skillet. Cover the skillet with a clean, damp cloth, and set it in a warm, draft-free place for 30 minutes.

3. Heat the oven to 350°F. Bake the bread in the skillet for 30 minutes, or until a toothpick inserted in the center comes out clean. Cool the bread in the skillet 10 minutes, then cut into wedges and serve warm.

BREADMATES: RICE AND SUCH

Cooked oatmeal, hominy grits, rice, mashed potatoes, and pureed pumpkin and squash can all be added to a basic country, savory, or even sweet bread. They add flavor, sweetness, and moisture and help create unusual texture. Rice lends moisture and a tender chewiness to the crumb. Pumpkin and other sweet squash also increase moisture as well as sweetness and oatmeal creates a substantial crumb.

To add any of these substances to your breads, substitute ½ cup of the new ingredient for ½ cup of the flour in the recipe. Stir the ingredient right into the dough and knead as usual.

Vermont Oatmeal Bread

....

This is one of our favorite sandwich breads. The addition of sweet whole oats fortifies the bread, turning a simple sandwich into a hearty whole meal.

MAKES 2 LOAVES

2 packages active dry yeast	2½ cups boiling water
½ cup warm water	4 to 5 cups all-purpose flour
(105° to 115° F)	1 cup whole-wheat flour
⅓ cup light molasses	1 cup instant nonfat dry milk
2 cups old-fashioned rolled oats	powder
3 tablespoons vegetable oil	½ cup soy flour
4 teaspoons salt	¼ cup wheat germ

1. In a small bowl, sprinkle the yeast over the warm water. Stir in the molasses and let the mixture stand until foamy, about 15 minutes.

2. In a large bowl, combine the oats, oil, salt, and boiling water. Cool to 105° to 115°F. Stir the yeast mixture into the oats mixture. In another large bowl, combine 4 cups all-purpose flour, the whole-wheat flour, milk powder, soy flour, and wheat germ. Stir the flour mixture into the oats mixture to make a soft, manageable dough. Turn onto a lightly floured surface and knead, working in as much of the remaining all-purpose flour as necessary, until the dough is smooth, about 10 minutes.

3. Shape the dough into a ball and place in a large, lightly oiled bowl, turning once to bring the oiled side up. Cover the bowl with a clean, damp cloth and set it in a warm, draft-free place until the dough has doubled in size, 40 to 45 minutes. Punch down the dough. Cover again and set in a warm, draft-free place until the dough has doubled in size, 40 to 45 minutes.

4. Grease two 9- by 5-inch loaf pans. Punch down the dough and divide it in half. Shape each half into an oblong loaf and place each in a prepared pan. Cover with clean, damp cloths and set in a warm, draft-free place until the loaves have doubled in size, 30 to 40 minutes.

5. Heat the oven to 425°F. Bake the loaves 15 minutes. Reduce the heat to 375°F and bake 30 minutes longer, or until the loaves are lightly browned and sound hollow when tapped on the top with a fingertip. Remove the loaves from the pans and cool completely on a wire rack.

Whole-Wheat Toasting Bread

....

Use stone-ground whole-wheat flour for an even wheatier flavor. Sliced for toasting, this is great for BLTs or served at breakfast with melting butter and preserves. Add ¼ cup raisins to the dough for a classic raisin bread.

MAKES 1 LOAF

1 package active dry yeast
¼ cup warm water
  (105° to 115° F)
1 tablespoon sugar
1 cup milk, scalded and cooled
  to 105° to 115° F

2 tablespoons vegetable shortening,
  softened
1 egg
1 teaspoon salt
3 to 3½ cups whole-wheat flour

1. In a large bowl, sprinkle the yeast over the water. Stir in the sugar and let stand until foamy, about 5 minutes. Stir the milk, shortening, egg, salt, and 1 cup flour into the yeast mixture. Beat with a wooden spoon until smooth. Gradually stir in enough of the remaining flour to make a soft, manageable dough. Cover the bowl with a clean, damp cloth and let the dough rest 30 minutes.

2. Turn the dough onto a lightly floured surface and knead, working in any of the remaining flour as necessary, until the dough is smooth and elastic, about 10 minutes. Shape the dough into a ball and place in a large, lightly oiled bowl, turning once to bring the oiled side up. Cover the bowl with a clean, damp cloth and set it in a warm, draft-free place until the dough has doubled in size, about 1 hour.

3. Grease an 8½- by 4½-inch loaf pan. Punch down the dough, shape it into an oblong loaf, and place it in the prepared pan. Cover with a clean, damp cloth and set it in a warm, draft-free place until the loaf has doubled in size, about 1 hour.

4. Heat the oven to 375°F. Bake the loaf 25 to 35 minutes, or until it sounds hollow when tapped on the top with a fingertip. Remove the loaf from the pan and cool completely on a wire rack.

Finnish Coffee Bread, page 62

Garlic Braid, page 50

Casterole Health Bread

....

For a wonderful gift, bake this in an antique or earthenware casserole. Unmold and cool the bread, then place it back in the casserole and wrap it all up for gift-giving.

MAKES 1 LOAF

2 packages active dry yeast
½ cup warm water
  (105° to 115° F)
1¼ cups milk, scalded and
  cooled to 100° F
¼ cup honey
¼ cup plus 1 tablespoon
  vegetable shortening, butter,
  or margarine

2 teaspoons salt
4 cups stone-ground
  whole-wheat flour
1¼ cups finely shredded carrots
1 cup dark seedless raisins
1½ to 2 cups all-purpose flour

1. In a large bowl, sprinkle the yeast over the water. Stir in the milk, honey, shortening, and salt into the yeast mixture and let stand until foamy, about 10 minutes.

2. Stir the whole-wheat flour, carrots, and raisins into the yeast mixture to make a soft, manageable dough. Turn onto a lightly floured surface and knead, working in as much of the all-purpose flour as necessary, until the dough is smooth and elastic, about 10 minutes.

3. Shape the dough into a ball and place in a lightly oiled 1-quart casserole or ovenproof bowl, turning once to bring the oiled side up. Cover the casserole with a clean, damp cloth and set it in a warm, draft-free place until the dough has doubled in size, about 45 minutes.

4. Punch down the dough and turn onto a clean, lightly floured surface. Reshape the dough into a smooth ball and place again in the casserole. Cover the casserole with the cloth and set it in a warm, draft-free place until the dough has doubled in size, about 30 minutes.

5. Heat the oven to 325°F (350°F if using earthenware). Bake the bread for 30 minutes, or until it sounds hollow when tapped on the top with a fingertip. Cool the bread in the casserole 10 minutes. Remove the bread from the casserole and cool completely on a wire rack.

Whole-Wheat Bread, Whole-Wheat Rolls, or Cottage Loaf

....

S lightly sweet with the wonderful nutlike flavor of wheat, this bread can be baked in pans, shaped into a freeform loaf or rolls. Sprinkle the top with the cracked wheat if you want the extra crunch and flavor of the wheat.

MAKES 2 LOAVES

1½ packages active dry yeast
1½ cups warm water
   (105° to 115° F)
1 teaspoon honey
5 cups whole-wheat flour
1 tablespoon light-brown sugar
1 teaspoon salt

1 tablespoon butter or
   margarine, melted
1 tablespoon lightly salted water
   (optional)
1 teaspoon cracked wheat or
   unprocessed bran (optional)

1. In a small bowl, sprinkle the yeast over ½ cup of the water. Stir in the honey and let the mixture stand 10 minutes.

2. In a large bowl, combine the flour, brown sugar, salt, and butter. Stir the yeast mixture and enough of the remaining 1 cup water into the flour mixture to make a firm dough. Turn onto a lightly floured surface and knead until the dough is smooth and elastic, 8 to 10 minutes.

3. Shape the dough into a ball and place in a large, lightly oiled bowl, turning once to bring the oiled side up. Cover the bowl with a clean, damp cloth and set it in a warm, draft-free place until the dough has doubled in size, about 1 hour.

4. Grease two 9- by 5-inch loaf pans. Punch down the dough and divide it in half. Shape each half into an oblong loaf and place each loaf in a prepared pan. If desired, brush the loaves with salted water and sprinkle with cracked wheat. Cover the pans with clean, damp cloths and set them in a warm, draft-free place until the dough has doubled in size, about 1 hour.

5. Heat the oven to 400°F. Bake the loaves 25 to 35 minutes, or until they are golden brown and sound hollow when tapped on the top with a fingertip. Remove from the pans and cool completely on wire racks.

Whole-Wheat Rolls Variation

....

Serve these warm with soup or a meal. Sliced in half, they make wonderful small sandwiches.

MAKES 16 ROLLS.

After the first rising of whole-wheat bread, punch down the dough and shape into 16 rolls. Place the rolls on a greased baking sheet. Cover the rolls with a clean, damp cloth and set them in a warm, draft-free place until doubled in size, 20 to 30 minutes. Heat the oven to 400°F. Bake the rolls 15 to 20 minutes, or until they are golden brown and sound hollow when tapped on the top with a fingertip. Cool the rolls completely on wire racks.

Cottage Loaf Variation

....

The cottage loaf, came to be in 17th-Century England as a way of baking double amounts of bread in a small oven. The piggyback design was popular among early American bakers, possibly for the same reason.

MAKES 2 LOAVES

After the first rising of whole-wheat bread, punch down the dough. Cut off a third of the dough and knead into a ball. Knead the remaining two thirds of the dough into a large round. Place the small ball on top of the large round. With the handle of a wooden spoon, press the knob through the center of the loaf to the bottom. Place the loaf on a greased baking sheet. Cover the loaf with a clean, damp cloth and set it in a warm, draft-free place until it has doubled in size, about 45 minutes. Heat the oven to 400°F. Lightly dust the loaf with flour and bake 25 to 30 minutes, or until it is golden brown and sounds hollow when tapped on the top with a fingertip. Cool the loaf completely on a wire rack.

Buttery Fantan Rolls

Fancy rolls, reminiscent of the supper clubs of the 1940s and 1950s, look and taste wonderful. You can make them up to 2 days ahead, and store them in airtight containers.

MAKES 3 DOZEN ROLLS

1 package active dry yeast
1½ cups warm water
   (105° to 115° F)
¼ cup sugar
5 to 5½ cups all-purpose
   flour

½ cup (1 stick) butter,
   softened
2 eggs
1 teaspoon salt
2 tablespoons milk

1. In a large bowl, sprinkle the yeast over ½ cup water. Stir in the sugar and let the mixture stand until foamy, about 5 minutes.

2. With a wooden spoon, stir 4½ cups flour, the remaining 1 cup water, ¼ cup butter, 1 egg, and the salt into the yeast mixture until smooth. Stir in enough of the remaining 1 to 1½ cups flour to make a soft, manageable dough. Turn onto a lightly floured surface and knead, working in as much of the remaining flour as necessary, until the dough is smooth and elastic, about 10 minutes.

3. Shape the dough into a ball and place in a large, lightly oiled bowl, turning once to bring the oiled side up. Cover the bowl with a clean, damp cloth and set it in a warm, draft-free place until the dough has doubled in size, 50 to 60 minutes.

4. Meanwhile, in a small bowl, beat the remaining egg and the milk. Set aside. In a small saucepan, melt the remaining ¼ cup butter over medium heat. Brush thirty-six 1½-inch muffin-pan cups with half the melted butter.

5. Punch down dough. On a lightly floured surface, roll out the dough into a 25-inch square. Brush the top with the remaining melted butter and then brush with half of the egg mixture. With a sharp knife cut the dough into twelve 1¼-inch-strips. Cut each dough strip crosswise in half. Stack 4 strips on top of one another and cut into 1¼-inch square squares. Repeat the process with the remaining strips.

6. Place the rolls, cut edge up, in the prepared muffin-pan cups. Cover the pans with clean, damp cloths, and set them in a warm, draft-free place until the rolls have doubled in size, 35 to 40 minutes.

7. Heat the oven to 350°F. Brush the tops of the rolls with the remaining egg mixture. Bake the rolls 25 minutes, or until golden brown. Cool the rolls completely on wire racks.

BREAD FOR MODERN SCHEDULES

Although we are partial to the old-fashioned, kneaded, double-rise yeasted breads, we are not in favor of becoming hostages to the process of baking bread at home. One does not have to spend the whole day in the kitchen in order to make a good loaf of bread. Ordinary yeast breads using active dry yeast can be baked at your convenience, accommodating hectic day-in, day-out schedules.

For fresh bread at dinner, mix and knead the dough in the morning. Cover and refrigerate it up to 10 hours. The cool temperature retards the lively activity of the yeast but doesn't stop it. The rising of the dough takes place at a very slow rate. Two or three hours before dinner, allow the dough to come to room temperature, shape the loaves, let them rise in a warm place, and bake according to directions.

If you like fresh bread in the morning, mix, knead, let rise, and shape the loaves before going to bed the night before. Place the loaves, covered, in the refrigerator overnight. The next morning allow about 2 hours for the loaves to come to room temperature and rise in a warm place. Then bake according to directions.

Coffee Rye Rolls

....

These little rolls are cousins to Dark Rye Bread (page 16). Molasses and coffee give them a bittersweet character that goes well with cream cheese at breakfast or with butter at dinner.

MAKES 1 DOZEN ROLLS

2 packages active dry yeast
1½ cups warm brewed
   chicory or regular coffee
   (105° to 115° F)
½ cup dark molasses
2¾ cups rye flour

2 tablespoons vegetable
   shortening
1 teaspoon salt
2 to 2½ cups all-purpose
   flour
2 to 3 tablespoons yellow
   cornmeal

1. In a large bowl, sprinkle the yeast over the warm coffee. Stir in the molasses and let the mixture stand until foamy, about 10 minutes.

2. Stir the rye flour, shortening, and salt into the yeast mixture until smooth. Stir in enough all-purpose flour to make a soft, manageable dough. Turn the dough onto a lightly floured surface and knead, working in as much of the remaining all-purpose flour as necessary, until the dough is smooth and elastic, about 10 minutes.

3. Shape the dough into a ball and place in a large, lightly oiled bowl, turning once to bring the oiled side up. Cover the bowl with a clean, damp cloth and set it in a warm, draft-free place until the dough has doubled in size, about 1 hour.

4. Grease a baking sheet and sprinkle it with the cornmeal. Punch down the dough and divide into 12 pieces. Shape each piece into a round ball and place on the prepared baking sheet. Flatten each ball slightly. Cover the baking sheet with a clean, damp cloth and set it in a warm, draft-free place until the rolls have doubled in size, 40 minutes.

5. Heat the oven to 375°F. Bake the rolls 20 to 25 minutes, or until they are lightly browned and sound hollow when tapped on the top with a fingertip. Remove the rolls from the baking sheet and cool completely on wire racks.

Clover Leaf Potato Rolls

....

Here is a classic soft dinner roll. Don't substitute leftover mashed potato for the freshly mashed potato in the recipe. If you wish, just before baking brush lightly with beaten egg and sprinkle with sesame or poppy seeds.

MAKES 16 ROLLS

1 large (½ pound) potato, peeled
  and cut into 1-inch chunks
1 cup warm water
  (105° to 115° F)
1 package active dry yeast

4½ to 5 cups all-purpose flour
¼ cup sugar
½ teaspoon salt
1 egg, lightly beaten

1. In a small saucepan, cook the potato in ½ cup of the water until tender, about 20 minutes. With a hand-held electric mixer on medium speed, beat the potato in the saucepan with the cooking liquid until it is well broken up. Cool to about 110°F.

2. In a small bowl, sprinkle the yeast over the remaining ½ cup water; let stand until dissolved. In a large bowl, combine 4 cups flour, sugar, and salt. Stir the potatoes, yeast mixture, and egg into the flour mixture to make a soft manageable dough. Knead in the bowl, working in more flour if necessary, until the dough forms a ball. Turn onto a lightly floured surface and continue kneading until the dough is smooth and elastic, about 10 minutes. Shape the dough into a ball and place in a large, lightly oiled bowl, turning once to bring the oiled side up. Cover the bowl with a clean, damp cloth and set it in a warm, draft-free place until the dough has doubled in size, about 45 minutes.

3. Grease and flour 16 muffin-pan cups. Punch down the dough and divide it into 16 pieces. Divide each piece into 3 pieces and shape into balls. Fit 3 balls into each muffin-pan cup. Cover the pans with clean, damp cloths, and set them in a warm, draft-free place, until the rolls have doubled in size, about 1 hour.

4. Heat the oven to 400°F. Bake the rolls 20 to 25 minutes, or until they are golden brown and sound hollow when tapped on the top with a fingertip. Cool the rolls in the pan 5 minutes. Remove the rolls and cool completely on wire racks.

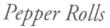

Pepper Rolls

Freshly ground black pepper gives these soft rolls their definite pepper taste, but you can experiment with green, red, or mixed peppercorns for a slightly different flavor.

MAKES 2 DOZEN ROLLS

5 to 5½ cups all-purpose flour
2 packages rapid-rising dry yeast
1 tablespoon freshly ground black
    pepper
1 tablespoon sugar
1 teaspoon salt

3 eggs
2 tablespoons butter or
    margarine, softened
1¼ cups very warm water
    (120° to 130° F)
Water

1. In a large bowl, combine 4 cups flour, the yeast, pepper, sugar, and salt. Separate 1 egg, reserving the yolk in a small cup.

2. Stir the egg white and remaining eggs, the butter and water into the flour mixture to make a soft, manageable dough. Knead the dough in the bowl, working in 1 cup of the flour until the dough is smooth. Turn onto a lightly floured surface and knead, working in as much of the remaining flour as necessary, until the dough is smooth and elastic, about 5 minutes.

3. Shape the dough into a ball and place on a lightly floured surface; cover with a clean, damp cloth and let it rest in a warm, draft-free place 20 minutes.

4. Grease 24 muffin-pan cups. Punch down the dough and divide it into 24 pieces. Shape each piece into a ball; place in the muffin-pan cup. Cover the pans with clean, damp cloths and set them in a warm, draft-free place until the rolls have doubled in size, 30 to 35 minutes.

5. Heat the oven to 350°F. Beat several drops of water into the reserved egg yolk. Brush some of the egg mixture over the rolls. Bake the rolls 20 to 25 minutes, or until they are golden brown and sound hollow when tapped on the top with a fingertip. Brush the rolls with the remaining egg mixture; bake 5 minutes longer, or until the egg is set. Remove the rolls from the cups and cool completely on a wire rack.

Zucchini Dinner Rolls

....

This extremely flavorful bread gets its lively tang from Parmesan cheese. It's terrific with soups, salads and pastas. Make a double batch and freeze the extras — you'll be glad you did.

MAKES 1 DOZEN ROLLS

1 cup coarsely grated zucchini	⅓ cup grated Parmesan cheese
½ teaspoon salt	1 cup very warm water
3½ cups all-purpose flour	(120° to 130° F)
1 package rapid-rising dry yeast	1 tablespoon vegetable oil
½ teaspoon sugar	

1. In a colander, combine the zucchini and salt. Set aside for 30 minutes. In a large bowl, combine 3 cups flour, the yeast, sugar, and all but 1 tablespoon of the cheese. Press the zucchini to drain well. Add the zucchini to the flour mixture, and toss to distribute evenly.

2. Stir the water and oil into the flour mixture to make a soft, manageable dough. Turn onto a lightly floured surface and knead, working in as much of the remaining flour as necessary, until the dough is smooth and elastic, about 10 minutes.

3. Shape the dough into a ball and place in a lightly oiled bowl, turning once to bring the oiled side up. Cover the bowl with a clean, damp cloth and set it in a warm, draft-free place for 20 minutes.

4. Grease 12 muffin-pan cups or a 9-inch-square baking pan. Punch down the dough and divide it into 12 pieces. For clover leaf rolls, divide each piece into thirds; shape into 3 balls and fit into a muffin-pan cup. For pan rolls, shape each of the 12 pieces into one ball and fit the balls into the square pan. Sprinkle the tops of the rolls with the reserved 1 tablespoon cheese. Cover the pan(s) with a clean damp cloth and set in a warm, draft-free place until the rolls have doubled in size, 40 minutes.

5. Heat the oven to 400°F. Bake the rolls 20 to 22 minutes for the clover leaf rolls or 25 to 28 minutes for the pan rolls, or until they are golden brown and sound hollow when tapped on the top with a fingertip. Remove the clover leaf rolls from the cups and cool completely on wire racks, or cool the pan rolls completely in the pan on a wire rack.

Whole-Grain Crescent Rolls

....

For the whole-grain enthusiast who doesn't want to give up the rich, buttery texture of croissants, these rolls are the best of both worlds. They have the classic delicate shape of the crescent and the heartier flavor of whole grain.

MAKES 32 ROLLS

½ cup milk
5 tablespoons butter or
   margarine, melted
1 package active dry yeast
½ cup warm water
   (105° to 115° F)
1 tablespoon sugar

2¼ to 2¾ cups all-purpose flour
2 cups whole-wheat flour
½ teaspoon salt
1 egg
1 teaspoon water
1 tablespoon caraway seeds

1. In a 1-quart saucepan, heat the milk until bubbles form around the side of the pan. Remove from the heat; stir in 3 tablespoons butter. Cool the mixture to 105° to 115°F.

2. In a large bowl, sprinkle the yeast over the warm water. Stir in the sugar and let the mixture stand until foamy, about 5 minutes. Stir 2¼ cups all-purpose flour, the whole-wheat flour, and salt into the yeast mixture until smooth. Stir the milk mixture into the flour mixture to make a soft, manageable dough. Turn onto a lightly floured surface and knead, working in as much of the remaining all-purpose flour as necessary, until the dough is smooth and elastic, about 10 minutes.

3. Shape the dough into a ball and place in a large, lightly oiled bowl, turning once to bring the oiled side up. Cover the bowl with a clean, damp cloth and set it in a warm, draft-free place until the dough has doubled in size, 1 hour.

4. Lightly grease 2 baking sheets. Punch down the dough and divide it into 4 pieces. Shape each piece into a ball. Flatten the balls into 8-inch rounds. With a sharp knife, cut each round into 8 triangles.

5. Brush the remaining 2 tablespoons butter over the tops of the triangles. Starting at the large end, roll up a triangle, jelly-roll style. Shape into a crescent and place, seam side down, on a prepared baking sheet. Repeat the process with the remaining triangles. Cover the rolls with clean, damp cloths and set them in a warm, draft-free place, 1 hour.

6. Heat the oven to 400°F. In a small bowl, beat the egg and 1 teaspoon water. Brush the tops of the rolls with the egg mixture. Press the caraway seeds into the tops of the rolls. Bake the rolls 15 to 20 minutes, or until lightly browned. Cool the rolls completely on wire racks.

SHAPING UP

Making our *Country Living* freeform breads requires that you know how to make just two basic shapes — round and long.

To shape dough into a round, either for a whole loaf or dinner rolls, place the dough or dough pieces on a lightly floured surface. Press it with the heel of your hand to force out any gas remaining from fermentation. Keeping the smooth side of the dough up, begin to rotate it tucking the sides under, towards the bottom center of the dough. Continue turning and tucking until you have a firm and smooth ball. The dough is then ready to proof on a board or baking sheet.

To shape a short loaf to be placed in a pan or a long loaf to be baked freeform, the technique is the same. Shape the dough into a round as above and then press with the fingertips into a rectangle. Fold the top 3 inches over and seal it to the dough using the heel of your hand. Fold down from the top and seal again. Seal the last seam on the bottom. For free-form loaves, gently roll the dough to elongate slightly. Place on a board or baking sheet to proof. (For a pan loaf, tuck the ends under and pinch to seal the dough closed. Place in the prepared pan.)

Peppered Squash Bread

....

This is a delicious moist bread with a hint of pepper. Butternut squash, pumpkin, even sweet potato can be substituted for the acorn squash. Because of the basket-weave shape, your dinner guests will want to break off hunks with their own hands. Let them!

MAKES 1 LOAF

4½ to 5½ cups all-purpose flour
¼ cup sugar
2 packages rapid-rising dry yeast
1½ teaspoons cracked black
  pepper
1 teaspoon salt
1 cup cooked acorn squash puree,
  warmed

6 tablespoons butter or
  margarine, softened
½ cup very warm water
  (120° to 130° F)
¼ cup milk, scalded and cooled
  to 120° to 130° F
1 egg
1 tablespoon water

1. In a large bowl, combine 4½ cups flour, the sugar, yeast, pepper, and salt. In a small bowl, combine the squash, butter, very warm water, and milk. Stir the squash mixture into the flour mixture to make a soft, manageable dough. Turn onto a well-floured surface and knead, working in as much of the remaining flour as necessary, until the dough is smooth and elastic, about 10 minutes.

2. Shape the dough into a ball and place in a large, lightly oiled bowl, turning once to bring the oiled side up. Cover the bowl with a clean, damp cloth and set it in a warm, draft-free place until the dough has doubled in size, 1 hour.

3. Grease a baking sheet. Punch down the dough and roll it out into a 10-inch square. With a sharp knife, cut the square into ten 10- by 1-inch strips. On the prepared baking sheet, lay 5 dough strips next to each other. Fold the first, third, and fifth strips three-quarters of the way back. Lay one remaining strip crisscrossing the unfolded strips. Unfold the strips and fold back the second and fourth bottom strips. Lay a new strip crisscrossing the bottom strip and unfold the second and fourth strips. Repeat until all the dough strips are woven into a thick weave. Pinch the ends of the strips together to seal. Cover the baking sheet with

a clean, damp cloth and set it in a warm, draft-free place until the bread has doubled in size, 40 minutes.

4. Heat the oven to 350°F. In a small bowl, beat the egg and 1 tablespoon water. Brush the top of the bread with the egg mixture. Bake the bread 30 to 40 minutes, or until it is well browned. Serve the bread warm, or cool completely on a wire rack.

PROBLEMS? WHAT HAPPENED?

The shaped loaf flattened out during proofing: Proofing is the final chance for the newly shaped loaf to rise before baking. If the dough is too soft ("slack" is the word for it) the loaf will not proof well. You may not have kneaded in enough flour.

One side is higher in the pan: Usually this is the fault of the oven. To ensure even baking, turn the pan 180 degrees after 15 to 20 minutes of baking.

The top of the pan bread cracked open: Some people like this look. As the bread expands, it breaks the crust unevenly. It doesn't damage the bread. If you want the break to be more regular, score the loaf down the center just before baking.

The bread is crumbly when I slice it: If the dough wasn't patiently kneaded to the smooth and elastic stage, the crumb of the final bread can fall apart. The taste is usually good. It's the texture that suffers. Too much liquid and not enough flour could also cause the crumble.

The interior crumb is too tough: The dough may have been underkneaded; it may not have risen fully enough; or it simply may have been overbaked.

Garlic Braid
PHOTOGRAPH ON PAGE 36

The aromatic braids of garlic we've seen hanging in Italian kitchens inspired this fantasy bread. It is lightly perfumed with garlic and is remarkably easy to shape and sculpt. Be sure to work on a well-greased baking sheet, and refer to the photograph as you assemble the braid. Serve at room temperature, drizzled with hot garlic butter.

MAKES 1 BRAID OR 1 LOAF

5 to 5½ cups all-purpose
flour
2 packages rapid-rising dry
yeast
2 tablespoons sugar
1½ teaspoons salt
1¾ cups very warm water
(120° to 130° F)
1 egg

2 tablespoons butter or
margarine, softened
2 cloves garlic, finely
chopped

Garlic Butter:
½ cup (1 stick) butter or
margarine
2 cloves garlic, finely chopped

1. In a large bowl, combine 4 cups flour, the yeast, sugar, and salt. Gradually stir in the water, egg, butter, garlic, and 1 cup of the remaining flour to make a soft, manageable dough. Knead in the bowl until the flour is incorporated. Turn onto a lightly floured surface and knead the dough, working in remaining flour as necessary, until it is smooth and elastic, about 10 minutes. Shape the dough into a ball on the work surface; cover with a clean, damp cloth and set it in a warm, draft-free place, for 30 minutes.

2. Grease a large baking sheet. Divide the dough into 25 equal pieces. Set aside 4 pieces. With your hands, roll each of the remaining 21 pieces into a teardrop shape with 3-inch tapering stem, to resemble a garlic bulb with a stem.

3. Starting at one end of the baking sheet, arrange 3 dough pieces in a triangle with the stems meeting at the top. Moisten the stems and press together. Add 2 more dough pieces above and touching the first pieces. Add another dough piece in the center, on top of the last 2. Moisten the stem and press onto other stems.

4. Continue adding pieces in the same manner to make a loaf about 14 inches long and 5 inches wide, resembling a garlic braid. With a

sharp knife, score dough pieces to resemble the cloves in a garlic bulb.

5. Roll 3 of the reserved pieces into 6-inch long ropes. Braid the ropes, moisten one end, and tuck under the top of the loaf.

6. Cut the remaining dough into 21 small pieces. Flatten each piece with your thumb. With a sharp knife, make 4 or 5 cuts to within ⅛-inch of one edge and flatten each piece. Moisten the uncut edges and press into the centers of the dough "bulbs," as pictured, to resemble roots.

7. Cover the loaf with a clean, damp cloth and set it in a warm draft-free place until the dough has doubled in size, 20 to 25 minutes.

8. Heat the oven to 375°F. Bake the loaf 25 to 30 minutes or until it sounds hollow when tapped on top with a fingertip. Remove the loaf from the baking sheet and cool completely on a wire rack. If desired, prepare Garlic Butter: in a small saucepan, melt the butter. Stir in the garlic. Drizzle on the loaf, or serve alongside loaf for dipping.

FINISHES

The look of the crust of your bread depends on the ingredients in the dough. The crust of a bread high in sugar will brown well; one made with water will be thick and crusty; one made with eggs and fat will be soft and golden. To ensure a shiny, golden crust, make an egg wash by beating 1 egg with 1 tablespoon of water. Brush the wash over the loaf just before baking. If you want a glossy crust without the deep golden color, apply a wash of egg white only.

Some rustic Old World breads can be enhanced by sprinkling cracked wheat, cracked rye, rolled oats, or even flour on the crust as the bread is proofing. These finishes add character to the look and crunch to the taste of the bread.

To bring extra flavor, texture, and an eye-catching finish to soft dinner rolls, brush lightly with an egg wash and sprinkle with sesame, poppy, or caraway seeds just before baking. Coarse salt can be sprinkled in the same way on savory rolls.

Herbed Potato-Cheese Bread

PHOTOGRAPH ON PAGE 18

The dough is baked around a tangy cheese filling. The result is perfect as an accompaniment for soups and salads.

MAKES 1 LOAF

1 cup plus 1 tablespoon milk
4½ to 5 cups all-purpose
flour
2 packages active dry yeast
1 tablespoon sugar
1 cup mashed potatoes
½ cup (1 stick) butter or
margarine, softened
1 teaspoon salt

1 pound mozzarella cheese,
cut into ¼-inch cubes
1 tablespoon fresh thyme
leaves
1 teaspoon chopped fresh
rosemary leaves
1 egg
1 teaspoon poppy seeds

1. In a small saucepan, heat 1 cup milk over medium heat until bubbles form around the side of the pan. Pour the milk into a large bowl and cool to 110° to 115°F. Stir 1 cup flour, the yeast, and sugar into the milk; let the mixture stand until foamy, about 20 minutes.

2. Stir 3 cups flour, the potatoes, butter, and salt into the yeast mixture to make a soft, manageable dough. Turn onto a lightly floured surface and knead, working in as much of the remaining flour as necessary, until the dough is smooth and elastic, 12 to 14 minutes. Shape the dough into a ball and place in a large, lightly oiled bowl, turning once to bring the oiled side up. Cover the bowl with a clean, damp cloth and set it in a warm, draft-free place until the dough has doubled in size, about 1 hour.

3. Grease a baking sheet. Punch down the dough and roll it into an 18-inch round. In a small bowl, combine the cheese, thyme, and rosemary; mound the cheese mixture in the center of the dough. Lift the edge of the dough and bring it to the center, allowing the dough to fold in a spiral over the cheese. Pinch the dough at the center to close and create a "topknot." Place the dough on the prepared baking sheet. Cover with a clean, damp cloth and set in a warm, draft-free place 45 minutes.

4. Heat the oven to 350°F. In a small bowl, beat the egg and 1 tablespoon milk. Brush the bread with the egg mixture and sprinkle with the poppy seeds. Bake the bread 55 to 60 minutes, or until it is golden brown. Cool the bread on a wire rack 20 minutes. Serve warm.

Focaccia (top & bottom), page 12; and Garlic Bread (center), page 61

Cheesy Wheat Bread, page 59

Country Dill Bread

....

What gives this batter bread its fresh taste is herbs fresh from the garden. And start to finish, it is ready to serve in just 1½ hours.

MAKES 1 LOAF

1¼ cups all-purpose flour
1 cup whole-wheat flour
1 package active dry yeast
2 tablespoons sugar
½ teaspoon salt
1 cup milk, scalded and cooled
  to 115° F

2 tablespoons snipped fresh dill
  or 1 teaspoon dried dillweed
1 tablespoon snipped fresh chives
  or freeze-dried chives
Milk for glazing (optional)
½ teaspoon dillseeds (optional)

1. In a medium-size bowl, combine ¼ cup all-purpose flour, ½ cup whole-wheat flour, the yeast, sugar, and salt.

2. With an electric mixer on medium speed, gradually beat the warm milk into the flour mixture. Add the dill and chives. With a wooden spoon, gradually stir in the remaining all-purpose flour and whole-wheat flour to make a stiff batter.

3. Grease an 8-inch cast-iron skillet or 8-inch round baking pan. Spoon the batter into the prepared skillet. Cover the skillet with a clean, damp cloth and set it in a warm, draft-free place until the batter has doubled in size, about 1 hour.

4. Heat the oven to 400°F. Lightly brush the top of the loaf with milk and sprinkle with dillseeds, if desired. Bake the loaf 20 to 30 minutes, or until it is golden brown and sounds hollow when tapped on the top with a fingertip. Cool the bread slightly in the skillet on a wire rack. Cut the bread into wedges and serve warm.

BREADMATES: HERBS

Herbs added to breads create lovely loaves full of taste and fresh bouquet. Crumbled dried herbs are intensely concentrated, so don't go overboard. Fresh herbs are less intense. To substitute fresh for dried herbs, use 3 teaspoons fresh for every 1 teaspoon dried.

Herb Garden Bread

S erved warm with butter, at room temperature with soft cheese, or toasted with garlic butter, this bread explodes with herb flavor.

MAKES 3 SMALL LOAVES

2 cups whole-wheat flour
1 cup all-purpose flour
1 package rapid-rising dry
   yeast
1 teaspoon salt
1 cup very warm water
   (120° to 130° F)
2 tablespoons olive oil
1 large clove garlic, pressed
   or minced

2 tablespoons chopped fresh
   parsley leaves
¼ teaspoon dried oregano
   leaves
½ teaspoon dried thyme
   leaves
½ teaspoon dried rosemary,
   crumbled
½ teaspoon dried tarragon

1. In a large bowl, combine the whole-wheat flour, ½ a cup all-purpose flour, the yeast, and salt. Stir the water and oil into the flour mixture to make a soft manageable dough. Turn onto a lightly floured surface and knead, working in as much of the remaining all-purpose flour as necessary, until the dough is smooth and elastic, about 10 minutes.

2. Shape the dough into a ball and place in a large, lightly oiled bowl, turning once to bring the oiled side up. Cover the bowl with a clean, damp cloth and set it in a warm, draft-free place until the dough has doubled in size, about 40 minutes.

3. Lightly grease a large baking sheet. Punch down the dough and knead in the garlic, parsley, oregano, thyme, rosemary, and tarragon. Divide the dough into 3 pieces and shape each into a ball. With well-greased hands, shape each ball into a 12-inch-long loaf (Shaping up, page 47). Place the loaves on the prepared baking sheet. Cover with a clean, damp cloth and set it in a warm, draft-free place until the loaves have doubled in size, about 25 minutes.

4. Heat the oven to 425°F. With a sharp knife, score the loaves by cutting 1 or 2 slits ¼-inch to ½-inch deep lengthwise on top. Bake the loaves 20 minutes, or until they are golden brown and sound hollow when tapped on the top with a fingertip. Cool the loaves completely on a wire rack.

Rye and Indian Bread

....

This is a dense bread with the pungent flavor of rye and the sweet taste of cornmeal and molasses. It bakes into a round, substantial country loaf, but don't expect it to rise high and lofty in the oven. Dust with a little extra rye flour just before baking.

MAKES 1 LOAF

1 package active dry yeast	*1 cup rye flour*
1 cup warm water	*1 cup yellow cornmeal*
(105° to 115° F)	*½ teaspoon salt*
2 cups all-purpose flour	*¼ cup light molasses*

1. In a small bowl, sprinkle the yeast over ½ cup warm water; let stand until dissolved, about 5 minutes.

2. In a large bowl, combine the all-purpose flour, rye flour, cornmeal, and salt. Stir the yeast mixture, the remaining ½ cup warm water, and the molasses into the flour mixture to form a soft, moist dough. Knead the dough in the bowl until it forms a ball. Turn onto a lightly floured surface and knead until the dough is smooth, 3 to 5 minutes.

3. Shape the dough into a ball and place in a large, lightly oiled bowl, turning once to bring the oiled side up. Cover the bowl with a clean, damp cloth and set it in a warm, draft-free place until the dough has doubled in size, about 45 minutes.

4. Grease and flour a 9-inch circle in the center of a baking sheet. Punch down the dough and shape into a ball. Place the ball on the prepared baking sheet; flatten the ball slightly and pierce the top several times with a fork. Cover the dough with a clean, damp cloth and set the baking sheet in a warm, draft-free place until the bread has doubled in size, 45 to 60 minutes.

5. Heat the oven to 350°F. Bake the bread 30 to 40 minutes, or until it is golden brown and sounds hollow when tapped on the top with a fingertip. Remove the bread from the baking sheet and cool completely on a wire rack.

Garlic-Onion Bread

This is a savory batter bread that bakes in a casserole. It is best served warm, cut into wedges.

MAKES 1 LOAF

2 tablespoons butter or
margarine
1 medium-size onion, sliced
2 cloves garlic, cut into
slivers
1 cup milk
1½ cups all-purpose flour

1 cup whole-wheat flour
1 package rapid-rising dry
yeast
1 tablespoon sugar
½ teaspoon salt
1 egg
Cornmeal

1. In a 2-quart saucepan, melt the butter over medium heat. Add the onion and garlic; cook until tender. With a slotted spoon, remove the onion mixture to a plate. Set aside. Add the milk to the saucepan; heat just until very warm (120° to 130°F).

2. In a large bowl, combine ½ cup all-purpose flour, ½ cup whole-wheat flour, the yeast, sugar, and salt. With an electric mixer on low speed, gradually beat the warm milk mixture into the flour mixture just until combined. Increase the mixer speed to medium, and beat in the egg and the remaining ½ cup whole-wheat flour. Beat the batter, scraping the bowl occasionally, 2 minutes longer.

3. With a wooden spoon, stir in enough of the remaining all-purpose flour to make a stiff batter. Cover the bowl with a clean, damp cloth and set it in a warm, draft-free place until the batter has doubled in size, about 30 minutes.

4. Grease an 8-inch round baking pan or casserole dish. Sprinkle the bottom lightly with cornmeal. Stir down the batter and spread it evenly in the prepared pan. Sprinkle the reserved onion mixture over the batter. Cover the pan with a clean, damp cloth and set it in a warm, draft-free place until the batter has doubled in size, about 25 minutes.

5. Heat the oven to 350°F. Bake the bread 25 minutes, or until it is golden brown and sounds hollow when tapped on the top with a fingertip. Cool the bread in the pan on a wire rack 10 minutes. Cut the bread into wedges and serve warm.

Cheesy Wheat Bread

PHOTOGRAPH ON PAGE 54

Frugal home bakers have always added bread crumbs or cracked wheat to breads to give them extra food value and taste. In this recipe, the extra bulgur and loads of Cheddar cheese make this a high-protein, high-taste bread.

MAKES 1 LOAF

2 cups all-purpose flour
1¼ cups whole-wheat flour
¼ cup bulgur
1 package rapid-rising dry
   yeast
1 teaspoon salt
1 teaspoon light brown sugar

1½ cups very warm water
   (120° to 130° F)
1 tablespoon butter or margarine, melted
1¾ cups shredded sharp
   Cheddar cheese

1. In a large bowl, with an electric mixer on low speed, beat 1 cup all-purpose flour, 1 cup whole-wheat flour, the bulgur, yeast, salt, brown sugar, very warm water, and butter just until combined. With a wooden spoon, beat in the remaining 1 cup all-purpose flour and ¼ cup whole-wheat flour to form a sticky dough. Cover the bowl with a clean, damp cloth and set in a warm, draft-free place until the dough is doubled in size, 30 to 45 minutes.

2. Lightly grease an 8-inch round baking pan. Punch down the dough and stir in 1 cup cheese. Turn the dough onto a lightly floured surface. Roll out the dough into an 18- by 8-inch rectangle. Place the rectangle so that the short edge faces you. Lightly mark the long edges of the dough into thirds. Sprinkle about half the remaining ¾ cup cheese over the center third of the dough. Fold the bottom third of the dough over the center and sprinkle with most of the remaining cheese. Fold over the top third. Press the dough around the edges to seal in the cheese. Shape the dough to fit into the prepared pan.

3. Cover the pan with a clean, damp cloth and set it in a warm, draft-free place until the dough has doubled in size, about 1¼ hours.

4. Heat the oven to 400°F. Sprinkle the remaining cheese over the top of the bread and bake the loaf 35 minutes, or until it is golden brown and sounds hollow when tapped on the top with a fingertip. Remove the bread from the pan and cool completely on a wire rack.

Assorted Breadsticks With Herb Butter

....

L ight and crispy with lots of poppy, sesame, and caraway seeds, these breadsticks are served with their own herb butter. Homemade breadsticks are a rare treat.

MAKES 5 DOZEN BREADSTICKS

6 to 6½ cups all-purpose
   flour
2 packages rapid-rising dry
   yeast
1 tablespoon sugar
1½ teaspoons salt
2 cups very warm water
   (120° to 130° F)
2 tablespoons olive or
   vegetable oil
1 egg white
2 tablespoons sesame seeds
2 tablespoons caraway seeds
2 tablespoons poppy seeds

2 tablespoons unprocessed
   bran

Herb Butter:
1 cup (2 sticks) butter,
   softened
2 tablespoons chopped green
   onions
2 tablespoons snipped fresh
   dill or ¼ teaspoon dried
   dillweed
2 tablespoons chopped fresh
   parsley leaves

1. In a large bowl, combine 6 cups flour, the yeast, sugar, and salt. Stir the water and oil into the flour mixture to make a soft, manageable dough. Knead in the bowl until smooth. Shape the dough into a ball and place on a lightly floured surface. Cover with a clean, damp cloth and let it rest 15 minutes.

2. Punch down the dough and lightly knead, working in as much of the remaining flour as necessary, until the dough is smooth, about 5 minutes.

3. Lightly grease 2 baking sheets. Divide the dough into 60 pieces. On a lightly floured surface, roll each piece into a 10-inch rope. Place about half the ropes, 1 inch apart, on the baking sheets. Place the remaining ropes on lightly greased pieces of aluminum foil cut to fit the baking sheets, (ready to be baked in a second batch).

4. Place the baking sheets and aluminum foil in a warm, draft-free place until the breadsticks have doubled in size, about 30 minutes.

5. Heat the oven to 350°F. In a small bowl, beat a few drops of water into the egg white. Brush the egg white mixture over the breadsticks.

Sprinkle the top of each stick with either sesame seeds, caraway seeds, poppy seeds, or bran. Bake the breadsticks 20 to 22 minutes, or until crisp and golden. Remove the breadsticks from the baking sheet and cool completely on wire racks. Place the remaining breadsticks, on the foil, onto the baking sheets. Bake as directed above, and cool.

6. Prepare the Herb Butter: In a small bowl, combine the butter, green onions, dill, and parsley. Spoon into a serving dish. Refrigerate the herb butter 30 minutes and serve with the breadsticks.

Garlic Bread

PHOTOGRAPH ON PAGE 53

Begin with a loaf of bread already purchased or baked — a crusty French or Italian loaf is best. Slice it, toast it, and dip it into the melted garlic herb butter. Make this at the last minute.

MAKES 8 PIECES

1 cup (2 sticks) butter or margarine
½ cup olive oil
3 cloves garlic, coarsely chopped
½ cup dry white wine
½ teaspoon ground black pepper
¼ teaspoon dried oregano leaves
2 tablespoons chopped fresh parsley leaves
2 12- to 14-inch loaves French bread

1. In a large skillet, melt the butter over medium heat. Stir in the oil and garlic. Cook over low heat 1 minute. Stir in the wine, pepper, and oregano. Heat the mixture to boiling over medium-high heat. Remove from the heat and stir in the parsley. Set aside.

2. Heat the broiler. Cut the French bread loaves lengthwise in half; cut each piece in half. (You should have 8 pieces.) Place the bread on a broiler pan; toast until golden brown. Dip the bread, cut side down, in the butter mixture; serve immediately.

Finnish Coffee Bread

PHOTOGRAPH ON PAGE 35

The perfect sweetness to begin the day or to pick up the afternoon, this robust cardamom-spiced braided loaf is topped with streusel and a sugar glaze. We recommend a heavy-duty mixer with a dough hook, but the bread can be hand kneaded instead.

MAKES 3 LOAVES

Dough:
2 cups milk
½ cup (1 stick) butter or margarine
2 packages active dry yeast
½ cup warm water (105° to 115° F)
1¼ cups sugar
4 eggs, lightly beaten
1¼ teaspoons ground cardamom
1 teaspoon salt
9½ to 10½ cups all-purpose flour

Streusel Topping:
2 tablespoons butter, softened
2 tablespoons all-purpose flour
2 tablespoons sugar

Glaze:
¼ cup water
2 tablespoons sugar
1 egg yolk

1. Prepare the Dough: In a 2-quart saucepan, heat the milk over medium heat just until bubbles form around the side of the pan. Remove from the heat. Stir in the butter. Cool the mixture to 100° F.

2. In a large bowl of a heavy-duty electric mixer, sprinkle the yeast over the warm water; let stand until dissolved, about 5 minutes.

3. With the mixer on low speed, beat the sugar, eggs, cardamom, salt, and cooled milk mixture into the yeast mixture. Gradually add 5 cups flour, beating after each 1-cup addition, until smooth. Let the mixture stand 10 minutes. Stir in 4½ cups flour until a soft dough forms.

4. With the electric mixer on medium speed and using a dough hook, knead the dough, adding as much of the remaining 1 cup flour as necessary, until the dough is smooth and elastic, about 7 minutes.

5. Shape the dough into a ball and place in a large, lightly oiled bowl, turning once to bring the oiled side up. Cover the bowl with a clean, damp cloth and set it in a warm, draft-free place until doubled in size, about 60 to 70 minutes.

6. Prepare the Streusel Topping: In a small bowl, with pastry blender or 2 knives, cut the butter into the flour and sugar until crumbly. Set aside.

7. Grease 3 baking sheets. Punch down the dough and divide into 9 balls. Roll each ball into a 14- to 15-inch rope. Braid 3 ropes to form a loaf; place the loaf on a prepared baking sheet. Repeat the process with the remaining dough. Cover the loaves with clean, damp cloths and set in a warm, draft-free place until the loaves have doubled in size, about 30 to 45 minutes.

8. Heat the oven to 325°F. Sprinkle the streusel topping down the center of the loaves. Bake the loaves 25 minutes, or until golden brown.

9. Meanwhile, prepare the Glaze: In a small bowl, beat the water, sugar, and egg yolk until combined. Brush some of the glaze over the loaves. Bake the loaves 5 minutes longer. Brush the loaves with the remaining glaze, and bake 5 minutes or until the loaves sound hollow when tapped on the top with a fingertip. Cool loaves completely on wire racks.

A W A R M , D R A F T - F R E E P L A C E

A lmost every fermenting dough spends at least 2 hours of its life covered and sitting in a warm, draft-free place, as the recipe dictates. There are a number of spots in the house that might provide a steady 80°F temperature:

- On top of the refrigerator. Most refrigerators are heat producers.
- On a high shelf in a cupboard in the kitchen. Heat rises and the top shelf of a cupboard is always warmer than the countertop.
- In a sunny window, as long as the window is closed and the dough is not subject to a draft.
- Near the water heater.
- On a sill next to a radiator (in winter).

Apple Pull-Apart Bread

....

At least two generations we know of have had fun making this bread. Also called monkey or bubble bread, it's a lumpy, silly-looking loaf, perfect for pulling apart in single servings.

MAKES 1 LOAF

1 cup milk
¼ cup dark seedless raisins
¼ cup (½ stick) butter or
* margarine*
3 to 3½ cups all-purpose
* flour*
½ cup sugar
1 package rapid-rising dry
* yeast*
½ teaspoon salt

1 egg
1 teaspoon vanilla extract
2 large Mutsu or Golden
* Delicious apples, peeled,*
* cored, and sliced length-*
* wise into eighths*
2 teaspoons lemon juice
½ teaspoon ground cinnamon
¼ teaspoon ground nutmeg
⅛ teaspoon ground cloves

1. In a 1-quart saucepan, heat the milk over medium heat until bubbles form around the side of the pan. Remove from the heat; add the raisins and 2 tablespoons butter. Set aside until the mixture cools to 120° to 130°F.

2. In a large bowl, combine 3 cups flour, ¼ cup sugar, the yeast, and salt. In a small bowl, lightly beat the egg and vanilla. Very gradually beat the milk mixture into the egg mixture. Stir the milk mixture into the flour mixture to make a soft dough. Turn onto a lightly floured surface and knead, working in as much of the remaining ½ cup flour as necessary, until the dough is smooth and elastic, about 10 minutes.

3. Shape the dough into a ball and place in a large, lightly oiled bowl, turning once to bring the oiled side up. Cover the bowl with a clean, damp cloth, and set in a warm, draft-free place, until the dough has doubled in size, about 30 minutes.

4. Grease and flour a 10-inch tube pan. Thinly slice each apple eighth crosswise. In a large bowl, toss the apples and lemon juice. In a small bowl, combine the remaining ¼ cup sugar, the cinnamon, nutmeg, and cloves.

5. Punch down the dough and divide it into 32 pieces. In a small saucepan, melt the remaining 2 tablespoons butter. Add the dough

pieces, sugar mixture, and butter to the apples. Toss to coat the dough pieces well. Place the mixture in the prepared pan. Set the pan, uncovered, in a warm, draft-free place, until the mixture has doubled in size, 35 to 40 minutes.

6. Heat the oven to 350°F. Bake the loaf 45 to 50 minutes, or until it is golden brown and sounds hollow when tapped on the top with a fingertip. Cool the loaf in the pan on a wire rack, 10 minutes. Remove from the pan and cool completely on the rack before serving. To serve, pull apart several sections of bread and apples.

STONE-GROUND FLOUR

When it comes to flour, fresh is best for flavor. Although the commercial flours available in supermarkets are fine for making breads, they can lose flavor during long shelf lives.

If you want to improve the taste of your breads, begin with the flour. Unbleached all-purpose flours such as the brands available in health and natural-food stores have not been treated with additives and are usually fresher and more flavorful.

Stone-ground whole-wheat flour and stone-ground unbleached flour are just about the freshest, most flavorful flours you can buy. They are milled according to a centuries-old method of grinding whole grain between two heavy stones. This stone milling is a slow, cool process, unlike the high-speed, high-heat, steel-roller milling of the commercial mills; because of the cool temperatures, no delicate B vitamins or minerals in the wheat are damaged in the process. Stone-ground whole-wheat flour contains the bran, germ, starch, and all the essential oils of the wheat grain. It's dark and feels moist and gritty to the touch, and it smells nutty and sweet. It is a perishable flour and should be used within a few weeks of purchase. Store in a cool, dry, place, in an airtight container.

Pear-Butter Bread

···········

This is so good and fruity, you'll want to bake two loaves. Thickly sliced and drenched in syrup, it makes a superb French toast.

MAKES 1 LOAF

Pear Butter:
8 medium-size (4 pounds)
   pears, peeled, cored, and
   chopped
¼ cup water
3 tablespoons light-brown
   sugar
2 teaspoons finely chopped
   peeled fresh gingerroot
1 teaspoon ground cinnamon
1 tablespoon lemon juice
1 package active dry yeast

½ cup warm water
   (105° to 115° F)
½ teaspoon granulated sugar
3 to 3½ cups all-purpose
   flour
2 eggs
¼ cup milk, scalded and
   cooled to 100° F
¼ cup vegetable oil
¼ cup honey
1 teaspoon salt

1. Prepare the Pear Butter: In a 4-quart saucepan, combine the pears, water, brown sugar, gingerroot, cinnamon, and lemon juice. Cook, covered, over medium heat, stirring occasionally, 45 minutes.

2. In a food processor fitted with the chopping blade, puree the pear mixture. Return the puree to the saucepan and cook over low heat until the mixture is thick and reduced to about 2 cups, 40 to 45 minutes. Cool the mixture to 100°F; cover and refrigerate until ready to use.

3. In a small bowl, sprinkle the yeast over the warm water. Stir in the granulated sugar and let the mixture stand until foamy, 5 minutes. Stir ½ cup flour into the yeast mixture. Cover the bowl with a clean, damp cloth and let stand for 30 minutes.

4. In a large bowl, combine the eggs, milk, oil, honey, and salt. Stir the yeast mixture and 2½ cups flour into the egg mixture to make a soft, manageable dough. Turn onto a lightly floured surface and knead the dough, working in as much of the remaining ½ cup flour as necessary, until the dough is smooth and elastic, about 10 minutes.

5. Shape the dough into a ball and place in a large, lightly oiled bowl, turning once to bring the oiled side up. Cover the bowl with a

clean, damp cloth and set in a warm, draft-free place until the dough has doubled in size, 50 to 60 minutes.

6. Grease a 9- by 5-inch loaf pan. Punch down the dough and divide it in half. Roll out one half into a 20- by 9-inch rectangle. Fit the dough into the prepared pan, allowing 5 inches of dough to overhang one long side. Spread ¼ cup pear butter on the bottom and sides of the dough-lined pan. Divide the remaining dough into 12 pieces. Alternately arrange the dough pieces and spoonfuls of ¾ cup of the pear butter in the pan. (Cover and refrigerate any remaining pear butter for another use.) Fold the overhanging dough over the filling and pinch to seal on the other side. Cover the loaf with a clean, damp cloth and set in a warm, draft-free place until the loaf has doubled in size, 40 to 50 minutes.

7. Heat the oven to 350°F. Bake the bread 45 to 50 minutes, or until it is lightly browned and sounds hollow when tapped on the top with a fingertip. Remove from the pan and cool completely on a wire rack.

S T O R I N G

Freshly made bread doesn't seem to last long enough in most households to have to worry about keeping it more than a couple of days.

Thick-crusted loaves, such as sourdough and dark rye, will keep lightly wrapped in a bread box for two or three days. It's best to store soft-crust breads and soft rolls in airtight containers, where they will keep well at room temperature for two or three days. Loaves filled with spicy meats, vegetables, and cheese should be kept covered and refrigerated. Warm them in a preheated 350°F oven for 20 minutes.

To freeze soft- or thick-crusted breads or rolls, wrap tightly in plastic wrap and freeze up to six months. Thaw in the wrapper. To refresh cold soft crust breads and rolls, sprinkle with a few drops water and wrap in aluminum foil. Place in a preheated 400°F oven for 10 minutes. To recrisp thawed thick-crusted breads, place in a preheated 350°F oven for 10 to 15 minutes.

The Della Robbia Wreath

....

This festive Christmas wreath, created by Judith Olney, is laden with
fruits and nuts and is much easier to make than the long list of ingredients seems to suggest. Decorate it any way you like; have all the ingredients set out in individual cups and bowls before you begin.

MAKES 1 LARGE WREATH

Wreath Dough:
1 package active dry yeast
¼ cup warm water
(105° to 115° F)
½ cup warm milk
(105° to 115° F)
3 tablespoons granulated
sugar
½ teaspoon salt
½ teaspoon ground cinnamon
2 tablespoons unsalted butter,
melted
1 egg, slightly beaten
2⅓ cups unbleached flour

Egg Glaze:
1 egg yolk, lightly beaten
1 teaspoon water
¼ teaspoon granulated sugar

Decoration:
2 candied pineapple slices,
thinly sliced

½ cup red candied cherries,
halved
¼ cup green candied cherries,
halved
4 candied orange slices
2 dried or candied pear
halves
4 prunes, soaked in water
overnight, drained
4 apricot halves, soaked in
water overnight, drained
Dates
Dark seedless and golden
raisins
Walnut halves
Hazelnuts
Whole almonds
Gold or silver dragées

Jelly Glaze:
½ cup red currant jelly
2 tablespoons water

Red sugar crystals

1. Prepare the Wreath Dough: In a large bowl, sprinkle the yeast over
the warm water; let stand until dissolved. Stir the milk, granulated sugar,
salt, cinnamon, butter, and egg into the yeast mixture until combined.
Add 1 cup flour and beat well for 5 minutes. Cover the bowl with a
clean, damp cloth and set it in a warm, draft-free place 40 minutes.

2. Stir down the batter. With a wooden spoon, stir in the remaining flour to make a soft, manageable dough. Turn onto a lightly floured surface and knead until the dough is smooth and elastic, about 10 minutes. Shape the dough into a ball. Cover the dough with plastic wrap and refrigerate for 30 minutes.

3. Grease a large baking sheet. On a lightly floured surface, roll out the dough into a 12-inch round. With a sharp knife, cut out a 6½-inch circle from the center of the round and set aside. Place the wreath-shaped dough on the prepared baking sheet.

4. Prepare the Egg Glaze: In a bowl, combine the egg yolk, water, and granulated sugar. Brush some of the egg glaze over the wreath.

5. For decoration, cover the surface of the dough wreath with the fruits and nuts. With a 2- or 3-inch leaf-shaped cookie cutter, cut leaf shapes from the reserved circle of dough. With a sharp knife, score the leaves with lines to resemble veins. Moisten the leaves with the egg glaze and press them into the wreath. Place a few gold or silver dragées randomly on the wreath for a gilding effect. Cover the wreath with a clean, damp cloth and set in a warm, draft-free place for 20 minutes.

6. Heat the oven to 350°F. Bake the bread 25 to 30 minutes, or until golden brown. Remove the bread from the oven, but leave it on the baking sheet. Heat the broiler.

7. Prepare the Jelly Glaze: In a small saucepan, heat the jelly and water over medium heat until melted. Brush the wreath with the jelly glaze and place the bread under the broiler briefly to glaze and gild the fruit. When the wreath has cooled 1 minute, sprinkle the top lightly with red sugar crystals. Cool the bread completely on the baking sheet.

IN THE OVEN

When baking two loaves, use a single rack in the center of the oven. If you have to use two racks for more than two loaves, rotate the breads halfway through baking to make sure they bake evenly.

Lemon Sesame Loaf

This is a zesty no-knead batter bread for the lemon lover. Just as the lemon-scented bread is taken from the oven, it is bathed with a lemon-infused syrup for extra moistness. It's perfect for afternoon tea or coffee, or sliced and served with vanilla ice cream for dessert.

MAKES 1 LOAF

2½ cups all-purpose flour
¾ cup sugar
½ cup sesame seeds, toasted
1 tablespoon baking powder
1 tablespoon grated lemon
  rind
¾ teaspoon salt
1¼ cups milk

½ cup vegetable oil
1 egg
2 teaspoons vanilla extract

Lemon Syrup:
¼ cup lemon juice
¼ cup sugar
1 teaspoon grated lemon rind

1. Heat the oven to 350°F. Grease an 8½- by 4½-inch loaf pan.

2. In a large bowl, combine the flour, sugar, sesame seeds, baking powder, lemon rind, and salt. In a small bowl, combine the milk, oil, egg, and vanilla. Stir the milk mixture into the flour mixture just until the flour mixture is moistened. Do not over mix. Spoon the batter into the prepared pan.

3. Bake the bread 55 to 60 minutes, or until a toothpick inserted in the center comes out clean. Prepare the Lemon Syrup: In a 1-quart saucepan, heat the lemon juice and sugar to boiling. Stir in the lemon rind; remove from heat. Make a series of toothpick holes in the top of the bread. Pour the lemon syrup over the bread. Cool the bread in the pan until all the syrup is absorbed, about 20 minutes. Remove the bread from the pan and cool completely on a wire rack.

Sweet Jammies, page 77

Bostonian Blueberry Muffins, page 81

Carrot-Honey-Date Muffins, page 75

Crunchy Oat and Cranberry Muffins, page 82

Pleasant Hill Squash Muffins

These are one of the reasons Pleasant Hill, a Shaker community in Kentucky, is so pleasant. Use butternut, acorn, or pumpkin squash for the best flavor and texture. The addition of chopped pecans and molasses gives these little cakes an autumn holiday character.

MAKES 1 DOZEN MUFFINS

½ cup (1 stick) butter or margarine, softened
½ cup firmly packed light-brown sugar
¼ cup light molasses
1 egg

1¼ cups cooked mashed squash
1¾ cups all-purpose flour
1 teaspoon baking soda
½ teaspoon salt
⅓ cup chopped pecans

1. Heat the oven to 375°F. Grease twelve 2½-inch muffin-pan cups.

2. In a large bowl, with an electric mixer on medium speed, beat the butter until light and fluffy. Beat in the sugar, molasses, egg, and squash until smooth.

3. Sift the flour, baking soda, and salt over the butter mixture. Stir just until combined. Stir in the pecans. Divide the batter among the prepared muffin-pan cups.

4. Bake the muffins about 20 minutes, or until they are lightly browned and the centers spring back when lightly pressed with a fingertip. Cool the muffins in the pan on a wire rack 5 minutes. Remove the muffins from the cups and serve warm.

MUFFIN BAKING TIP

When there isn't enough batter for all the muffin cups, fill the empties about ¾ full with water. This provides for even baking, keeps the unused cups from burning, and creates steam, which improves the texture of the muffins.

Apple Muffins

These compact little treasures are studded with chunks of tender apple in a honey-sweet, cinnamon crumb. Leave the red peel on the apple for color and texture.

MAKES 10 MUFFINS

Nut Topping:
3 tablespoons coarsely chopped
walnuts
2 tablespoons sugar
¼ teaspoon ground cinnamon

1 cup all-purpose flour
1 cup whole-wheat flour
¼ cup oat bran
2 teaspoons baking powder

1 teaspoon ground cinnamon
½ teaspoon baking soda
½ teaspoon salt
½ cup milk
⅓ cup honey
¼ cup (½ stick) butter or
margarine, melted
2 eggs
2 small red baking apples

1. Heat the oven to 400°F. Grease ten 2½-inch muffin-pan cups.

2. Prepare the Nut Topping: In a small bowl, combine the walnuts, sugar, and cinnamon. Set aside.

3. In a large bowl, combine the all-purpose flour, whole-wheat flour, oat bran, baking powder, cinnamon, baking soda, and salt. In a medium-size bowl, combine the milk, honey, butter, and eggs. Cut one ½-inch-thick slice from the side of each apple and reserve. Core and cut enough of the remaining apples into ¼-inch cubes to measure about 1 cup. Fold the apple cubes into the flour mixture. Stir the milk mixture into the flour mixture just until the flour mixture is moistened. Divide the batter among the prepared muffin-pan cups.

4. Cut the reserved apple slices crosswise into ⅛-inch-thick slices; insert 2 or 3 slices into the top of each muffin; sprinkle with the nut topping. Bake the muffins 20 to 25 minutes, or until they are golden brown and the centers spring back when lightly pressed with a fingertip. Remove the muffins from the cups and cool completely on wire racks.

Carrot-Honey-Date Muffins
PHOTOGRAPH ON PAGE 72

Whole-wheat flour results in a delightful, good-for-you taste. Dicing the dates can be a sticky mess; sprinkle them with flour first, or use a sharp knife which has been warmed with hot water.

MAKES 1 DOZEN MUFFINS

1 cup all-purpose flour
1 cup whole-wheat flour
1 tablespoon baking powder
1 teaspoon salt
½ cup milk
½ cup honey

¼ cup (½ stick) butter or
  margarine, melted
2 eggs
1 tablespoon finely grated
  orange rind
1 cup grated carrot
1 cup diced pitted dates

1. Heat the oven to 425°F. Grease twelve 2½-inch muffin-pan cups.

2. In a large bowl, combine the all-purpose flour, whole-wheat flour, baking powder, and salt. In a small bowl, combine the milk, honey, butter, eggs, and orange rind. Stir the milk mixture into the flour mixture just until the flour mixture is moistened. Stir in the carrot and dates. Divide the batter among the prepared muffin-pan cups.

3. Bake the muffins 15 to 20 minutes, or until a toothpick inserted in the centers comes out clean. Cool the muffins in the pan on a wire rack 5 minutes. Remove the muffins from the cups and serve warm.

NEXT-DAY MUFFINS

Store muffins after they have fully cooled. Wrap them tightly in plastic and store them in a cool place up to two or three days. Muffins baked in paper cup liners tend to stay fresher than those baked plain in the cup. If you want to perk up the taste of stored muffins, place them in a covered ovenproof pan in a preheated 350°F oven 15 minutes. Or sprinkle them with a few drops of water, wrap loosely with aluminum foil, and place them in a preheated 350°F oven 15 minutes.

Cheddar-Apple Muffins

We love these so much that we make them in giant-size, 7-ounce molds. To make the smaller 2½-inch muffins, cut the cheese into ¾-inch cubes and coarsely shred the remaining cheese for garnish. Bake 20 minutes.

MAKES 6 LARGE MUFFINS

¼ pound sharp Cheddar
  cheese
2¼ cups all-purpose flour
1 tablespoon baking powder
1½ teaspoons ground
  cinnamon
¼ teaspoon salt
1 large red cooking apple,
  unpeeled, cored, and
  coarsely shredded

½ cup chopped walnuts
⅔ cup milk
⅓ cup butter or margarine,
  melted
⅓ cup maple syrup
1 egg

1. Heat the oven to 375°F. Grease and flour six 7-ounce pottery cups; place on a rimmed baking sheet. Cut the cheese into six 1½- by ¾- by ¾-inch sticks. Coarsely shred any remaining cheese.

2. In a large bowl, combine the flour, baking powder, cinnamon, and salt. Add the apple and walnuts; toss to mix well. In a small bowl, combine the milk, butter, and syrup. Beat in the egg. Stir the milk mixture into the flour mixture just until the flour mixture is moistened.

3. Divide half the batter among the prepared cups; insert a cheese stick upright in the center of each. Fill the cups with the remaining batter, covering the cheese. (The cups will be full.) Sprinkle the reserved shredded cheese over the muffins.

4. Bake the muffins 30 to 35 minutes, or until they are golden brown and the centers spring back when lightly pressed with a fingertip. Cool the muffins in the pan 5 minutes. Remove the muffins from the cups and serve warm.

Sweet Jammies

PHOTOGRAPH ON PAGE 71

Your favorite jam or preserve is baked into the center of these classic American muffins. The contrast of the sweet fruit and tangy yogurt makes them habit forming.

MAKES 1 DOZEN MUFFINS

2 cups all-purpose flour
¼ cup granulated sugar
1 tablespoon baking powder
½ teaspoon baking soda
½ teaspoon salt
1 cup plain yogurt
¼ cup milk

¼ cup (½ stick) butter or
   margarine, melted
1 egg
½ teaspoon vanilla extract
About ¼ cup jam or preserves

Confectioners' sugar (optional)

1. Heat the oven to 425°F. Grease twelve 2½-inch muffin-pan cups.

2. In a large bowl, combine the flour, granulated sugar, baking powder, baking soda, and salt. In a medium-size bowl, combine the yogurt, milk, and butter. Stir in the egg and vanilla. Stir the yogurt mixture into the flour mixture just until the flour mixture is moistened.

3. Divide half the batter among the prepared muffin-pan cups. Place about 1 teaspoon jam on the batter in each cup. Top the cups with the remaining batter.

4. Bake the muffins 15 to 20 minutes, or until they are golden and the centers spring back when lightly pressed with a fingertip. Cool the muffins in the pan on a wire rack 5 minutes. Remove the muffins from the cups. Sprinkle with confectioners' sugar, if desired, and serve.

MUFFIN CUPS

We suggest using 2½-inch muffin-pan cups, 3-inch molds, 6-ounce custard cups, and 7-ounce molds for our various muffin recipes. Always grease the cups very well or line them with paper cup-liners. If you have nonstick-coated pans, grease them as well, just to guarantee their nonstick promises.

Raspberry Streusel Muffins

D efinitely special-occasion muffins, these taste as good as they look. They are bursting with a lively raspberry flavor, which contrasts wonderfully with the cinnamon-oat streusel topping. For those you love, bake them in heart-shaped molds.

MAKES 1 DOZEN MUFFINS

Streusel Topping:
½ cup all-purpose flour
½ cup quick rolled oats
⅓ cup granulated sugar
½ teaspoon ground
   cinnamon
⅛ teaspoon salt
6 tablespoons butter or
   margarine

½ cup (1 stick) butter or
   margarine, softened
½ cup granulated sugar

1 egg
2 cups all-purpose flour
½ teaspoon baking powder
½ teaspoon baking soda
½ teaspoon ground cinnamon
¼ teaspoon salt
½ cup milk
½ cup sour cream
1 teaspoon vanilla extract
1 cup fresh or drained
   thawed frozen raspberries

Confectioners' sugar

1. Heat the oven to 400°F. Grease twelve 3-inch heart-shaped muffin-pan cups or twelve 3-inch muffin-pan cups.

2. Prepare the Streusel Topping: In a medium-size bowl, combine the flour, oats, sugar, cinnamon, and salt. With a pastry blender or 2 knives, cut the butter into the flour mixture until the mixture resembles coarse crumbs. Briefly rub the mixture between your fingers to blend in the butter. Set aside.

3. In a large bowl, with an electric mixer on medium speed, beat the ½ cup butter and ½ cup sugar until light and fluffy. Add the egg, beating until well mixed.

4. In a medium-size bowl, combine the flour, baking powder, baking soda, cinnamon, and salt. In a small bowl, combine the milk, sour cream, and vanilla. With the mixer on low speed, and beginning and ending with the flour mixture, alternately beat the flour mixture and the milk into the butter mixture just until combined. Gently fold in the raspberries.

5. Divide the batter among the prepared muffin-pan cups, filling each about ⅔ full. Generously sprinkle the streusel topping over the muffins. (Any remaining streusel topping can be frozen and used to top pies, baked fruit, or other muffins.)

6. Bake the muffins 20 to 25 minutes, or until a toothpick inserted in the centers comes out clean. Cool the muffins in the pans on a wire rack 5 minutes. Remove the muffins from the cups. Sprinkle with confectioners' sugar and serve.

THE PERFECT MUFFIN

Fresh from the oven, a perfectly baked muffin has a rough, slightly rounded top, and is golden or dark brown in color. During baking, the muffin shrinks away from the sides of the muffin-pan cup. While it is hot, the muffin tends to be fragile. The inner crumb will be moist and almost cakelike, and the texture might be slightly crumbly. Plan to serve muffins warm for breakfast or as a substitute for bread at lunch, snack, or dinner.

• Mix muffin batters only until the ingredients are combined. Don't overmix; stirring the batter too much is the number one reason for muffins with mountainous volcanolike tops.

• Don't double the recipe.

• Move quickly from mixing bowl to pan.

• Fill the cups ⅔ full.

• Leave the hot muffins in the cups 5 minutes before unmolding.

• Allow muffins to cool like bread on a rack.

Pear-Hazelnut Muffins

....

Toasting the nuts lightly adds an intense flavor to these rich and sweet little cakes. This recipe makes the giant size, but if you want to make standard muffins, divide the batter among twelve 2½-inch greased muffin-pan cups. Bake in a preheated 400°F oven for 20 minutes.

MAKES 6 LARGE MUFFINS

½ cup hazelnuts
2¼ cups all-purpose flour
1 tablespoon baking powder
¼ teaspoon salt
1 cup coarsely shredded,
   unpeeled, cored firm Bosc or
   Bartlett pear (1 pear)

1 teaspoon finely grated lemon
   rind
⅔ cup milk
⅓ cup butter or margarine,
   melted
⅓ cup honey
1 egg

1. Heat the oven to 375°F. Grease six 6-ounce custard cups; place the cups on a rimmed baking sheet or jelly-roll pan.

2. Spread the hazelnuts in a shallow baking pan. Bake the hazelnuts 15 minutes, or until lightly toasted, shaking the pan once. Cool the hazelnuts completely. With a cloth towel or paper towels, rub the skins off the nuts. Coarsely chop the nuts.

3. In a large bowl, combine the flour, baking powder, and salt. Add the pear, lemon rind, and hazelnuts; toss to mix well.

4. In a small bowl, combine the milk, butter, and honey. Beat in the egg. Stir the milk mixture into the flour mixture just until the flour mixture is moistened. Divide the batter among the prepared custard cups. (The cups will be full.)

5. Bake the muffins 30 to 35 minutes, or until a toothpick inserted in the centers comes out clean. Cool the muffins in the cups on a wire rack for 5 minutes. Remove the muffins from the cups and serve warm.

Bostonian Blueberry Muffins

PHOTOGRAPH ON PAGE 71

The folks of Boston have been baking with blueberries since the 18th Century. These are hearty muffins and sweeter than many of the other blueberry versions. The uncomplicated burst of blueberry flavor makes them wonderful breakfast muffins.

MAKES 1 DOZEN MUFFINS

1 cup all-purpose flour
1 cup whole-wheat flour
½ cup plus 1½ tablespoons sugar
1 tablespoon baking powder
½ teaspoon salt
½ teaspoon ground cinnamon

1½ cups fresh or unthawed
  frozen blueberries
½ cup milk
½ cup (1 stick) butter or
  margarine, melted
2 eggs
½ teaspoon vanilla extract

1. Heat the oven to 425°F. Grease twelve 2½-inch muffin-pan cups.

2. In a large bowl, combine the all-purpose flour, whole-wheat flour, ½ cup sugar, the baking powder, salt, and cinnamon. In a small bowl, toss 1 tablespoon of the flour mixture with the blueberries. Set aside.

3. In another small bowl, combine the milk, butter, eggs, and vanilla. Stir the milk mixture into the flour mixture just until the flour mixture is moistened. Fold in the blueberries. Divide the batter among the prepared muffin-pan cups. Sprinkle the remaining 1½ tablespoons sugar over the muffins.

4. Bake the muffins about 15 minutes, or until they are golden brown and the centers spring back when lightly pressed with a fingertip. Cool the muffins in the pan on a wire rack 5 minutes. Remove the muffins from the cups and serve warm, or cool completely on a wire rack.

Crunchy Oat and Cranberry Muffins

PHOTOGRAPH ON PAGE 72

Old-fashioned rolled oats and plump whole cranberries create an irresistible crunchy, toothsome combination. If you're using frozen cranberries, add them as is. Don't thaw. Serve these warm with cinnamon butter.

MAKES 1 DOZEN MUFFINS

1 cup old-fashioned rolled oats
¾ cup all-purpose flour
¾ cup whole-wheat flour
½ cup firmly packed light-brown sugar
1 tablespoon baking powder
1 teaspoon salt

1 teaspoon ground cinnamon
1 cup fresh or unthawed frozen cranberries
1 cup milk
¼ cup (½ stick) butter or margarine, melted
1 egg

1. Heat the oven to 425°F. Grease twelve 2½-inch muffin-pan cups.

2. In a large bowl, combine the oats, all-purpose flour, whole-wheat flour, sugar, baking powder, salt, and cinnamon. In a small bowl, toss 1 tablespoon of the oats mixture with the cranberries. Set aside.

3. In another small bowl, combine the milk, butter, and egg. Stir the milk mixture into the oats mixture just until the oats mixture is moistened. Fold in the cranberries. Divide the batter among the prepared muffin-pan cups.

4. Bake the muffins 15 to 20 minutes, or until they are lightly browned and the centers spring back when lightly pressed with a fingertip. Cool the muffins in the pan on a wire rack 5 minutes. Remove the muffins from the cups and serve warm.

FROM MUFFINS TO BREAD

A recipe for twelve muffins baked in standard 2½-inch muffin-pan cups will easily make one quick bread. Grease a loaf pan, 8- by-4-inches, or a pan 8-inches square and fill it with the muffin batter. Bake at the same temperature as the muffins, and add about 10 minutes to the baking time.

Apple Muffins With Corn Bran

T hese make wonderful breakfast muffins. They are a rich, dense, and sweet marriage of corn and apple flavors in the crumb. A sprinkling of the corn bran-poppy seed topping adds a sweet crunch.

MAKES 8 MUFFINS

1 cup corn bran	⅓ cup light olive, canola, or
1¼ cups all-purpose flour	rice-bran oil
1 tablespoon baking powder	2 egg whites or 1 egg
¼ teaspoon ground allspice	½ cup chopped apple
1 cup skim milk	⅓ cup chopped pitted prunes
⅓ cup honey	4 teaspoons poppy seeds

1. Heat the oven to 400°F. Grease eight 2½-inch muffin-pan cups.

2. In a small bowl, reserve 1 tablespoon corn bran. In a large bowl, combine the flour, the remaining corn bran, the baking powder, and all-spice. In another small bowl, combine the milk, honey, oil, and egg whites. Stir the milk mixture into the flour mixture just until the flour mixture is moistened. Fold in the apple, prunes, and 2 teaspoons poppy seeds.

3. Divide the batter among the prepared muffin-pan cups. Combine the remaining 2 teaspoons poppy seeds and the reserved 1 tablespoon corn bran; sprinkle evenly over the muffins.

4. Bake the muffins 20 to 25 minutes, or until they are golden and the centers spring back when lightly pressed with a fingertip. Cool the muffins in the pan on a wire rack 5 minutes. Remove the muffins from the cups and serve warm.

THE BEST APPLE

O ur favorite apple for baking is Granny Smith. Choose apples that are firm, with a bright, even color and no bruises or soft spots.

Banana-Date-Nut Muffins

....

Besides being good for you, oat bran brings a natural sweetness and nutty texture to these muffins. You needn't wait until you have over-ripe fruit — any banana will do.

MAKES 8 MUFFINS

1¼ cups oat bran
1 cup all-purpose flour
1 tablespoon baking powder
¼ teaspoon ground cinnamon
¾ cup skim milk
¼ cup light olive, canola, or rice-bran oil

1 tablespoon honey
2 egg whites or 1 egg
¾ cup coarsely chopped banana
⅓ cup pitted dates, chopped
¼ cup chopped walnuts

1. Heat the oven to 400°F. Grease eight 2½-inch muffin-pan cups.

2. In a large bowl, combine the oat bran, flour, baking powder, and cinnamon. In a small bowl, combine the milk, oil, honey, and egg whites. Stir the milk mixture into the flour mixture just until the flour mixture is moistened. Fold in the banana and dates.

3. Divide the batter among the prepared muffin-pan cups. Sprinkle the walnuts over the muffins.

4. Bake the muffins 15 to 20 minutes, or until they are golden and the centers spring back when lightly pressed with a fingertip. Cool the muffins in the pan on a wire rack 5 minutes. Remove the muffins from the cups and serve warm.

KEEPING FLOUR FRESH

All-purpose flour, even with its long shelf life, must be stored in a dry, dark, moderately cool place, protected from high heat. A cupboard or old-fashioned flour bin is fine. Whole-wheat and stone-ground flours must be stored in the refrigerator because of the essential oils that have not been processed out of the flour. They will keep up to 3 months.

Corn Muffins

Here are quick, good-tasting muffins that pop out of the microwave in 3½ minutes. Microwave-safe muffin-pan cups and paper cup-liners are available at cookware stores.

MAKES 6 MUFFINS

½ cup all-purpose flour
½ cup yellow cornmeal
½ teaspoon baking soda
⅛ teaspoon salt

½ cup lowfat yogurt
2 tablespoons canola oil
2 tablespoons maple syrup
1 egg white, well beaten

1. Line six 2½-inch microwave-safe muffin-pan cups with large paper baking cups. In a medium-size bowl, combine the flour, cornmeal, baking soda, and salt. Stir in the yogurt, oil, and syrup just until combined. Gently fold in the egg white.

2. Divide the batter among the prepared muffin-pan cups. Microwave the muffins on high (100 percent) 2½ to 3½ minutes, or until a toothpick inserted in the centers comes out clean and the tops are almost dry. (Rotate the muffin pan midway if the microwave oven does not have a carousel.) Cool the muffins in the pan on a wire rack, 5 minutes. Remove the muffins from the cups and remove the paper baking cups. Serve the muffins warm, or cool completely on a wire rack.

ELECTRIC MIXER DOUGH

To knead the dough with the help of an electric mixer, combine the ingredients for the dough (except the flour) in the bowl of a heavy-duty electric mixer. With the mixer on low speed, beat with the paddle attachment until ingredients are well mixed. Change to the dough hook. With the mixer on low speed, beat in all but 1 cup of the flour. Stop the machine and scrape down the sides of the bowl. With the mixer on medium speed continue beating, adding more flour if the dough remains sticky. The dough is kneaded when it cleans the sides of the bowl and springs back when pressed with a fingertip, which usually takes 8 to 10 minutes.

Equivalents Table

....

EQUIVALENTS FOR COMMON INGREDIENTS

Flour, unsifted	2½ ounces	½ cup
	3½ ounces	¾ cup
	5 ounces	1 cup
Sifted	2½ ounces	¾ cup
Whole-wheat flour, unsifted	5½ ounces	1 cup
Rye flour	5½ ounces	1 cup
Cornmeal	4 ounces	¾ cup
Yeast, active or rapid-rising	1 package	1 tablespoon
Granulated sugar	1 pound	2 cups
Brown sugar	1 pound	2¼ cups
Confectioners' sugar	1 pound	4 cups
Walnuts, chopped	4 ounces	¾ cup
Almonds, whole	5⅓ ounces	1 cup
Unblanched, slivered	1 pound	3½ cups
Butter	½ ounce	1 tablespoon (⅛ stick)
	2 ounces	4 tablespoons (½ stick)
	4 ounces	8 tablespoons (1 stick)
Egg whites	8 to 10	1 cup

MEASURING EQUIVALENTS

3 teaspoons	1 tablespoon
8 tablespoons	½ cup
16 tablespoons	1 cup
1 liquid ounce	2 tablespoons
4 liquid ounces	½ cup
2 cups	1 pint
4 cups	1 quart
4 quarts	1 gallon
1 pound	16 ounces

Conversions Table

....

WEIGHTS		TEMPERATURES	
OUNCES & POUNDS	METRIC EQUIVALENTS	°F (FAHRENHEIT)	°C (CENTIGRADE OR CELSIUS)
¼ ounce	7 grams	32 (water freezes)	0
⅓ ounce	10 grams	108-110 (warm)	42-43
½ ounce	14 grams	140	60
1 ounce	28 grams	203 (water simmers)	95
1¾ ounces	50 grams	212 (water boils)	100
2 ounces	57 grams	225 (very slow oven)	107.2
2⅔ ounces	75 grams	245	120
3 ounces	85 grams	266	130
3½ ounces	100 grams	300 (slow oven)	149
4 ounces (¼ pound)	114 grams	350 (moderate oven)	177
6 ounces	170 grams	375	191
8 ounces (½ pound)	227 grams	400 (hot oven)	205
9 ounces	250 grams	425	218
16 ounces (1 pound)	464 grams	450	232
1.1 pounds	500 grams	500 (very hot oven)	260
2.2 pounds	1,000 grams (1 kilogram)		

LIQUID MEASURES

tsp.: teaspoon
Tbs.: tablespoon
8 ounces = 1 cup

U.S. SPOONS & CUPS	METRIC EQUIVALENTS	U.S. SPOONS & CUPS	METRIC EQUIVALENTS
1 tsp.	5 milliliters	⅓ cup + 1 Tbs.	1 deciliter (100 milliliters)
2 tsp.	10 milliliters	1 cup	240 milliliters
3 tsp. (1 Tbs.)	15 milliliters	1 cup + 1¼ Tbs.	¼ liter
3⅓ Tbs.	½ deciliter (50 milliliters)	2 cups	480 milliliters
¼ cup	60 milliliters	2 cups + 2½ Tbs.	½ liter
⅓ cup	85 milliliters	4 cups	960 milliliters
		4⅓ cups	1 liter (1,000 milliliters)

Index

Apple Muffins ~~~~~~~~~~~~~~~~~74
Apple Muffins with
  Corn Bran ~~~~~~~~~~~~~~~~83
Apple Pull-Apart Bread ~~~~~~~~~64
Assorted Breadsticks With
  Herb Butter ~~~~~~~~~~~~~~60

Banana-Date-Nut Muffins ~~~~~~84
Bostonian Blueberry Muffins ~~~~81
Braided Country Loaf ~~~~~~~~~~26
Buttery Fantan Rolls ~~~~~~~~~~40

Carrot-Honey-Date Muffins ~~~75
Casserole Health Bread ~~~~~~~~~37
Cheddar-Apple Muffins ~~~~~~ 76
Cheesy Wheat Bread ~~~~~~~~~~59
Clover Leaf Potato Rolls ~~~~~~ 43
Coffee Rye Rolls ~~~~~~~~~~~~~~42
Corn Light Bread ~~~~~~~~~~~~~32
Corn Muffins ~~~~~~~~~~~~~~~85
Country Dill Bread ~~~~~~~~~~~~55
Crunchy Oat and
  Cranberry Muffins ~~~~~~~~~82

Dark Rye Bread ~~~~~~~~~~~~~16
Della Robbia Wreath, The ~~~~68

Finnish Coffee Bread ~~~~~~~~~62
Focaccia ~~~~~~~~~~~~~~~~~~~12
Fougassette ~~~~~~~~~~~~~~~~~20

Garlic Braid ~~~~~~~~~~~~~~~~50
Garlic Bread ~~~~~~~~~~~~~~~~61
Garlic-Onion Bread ~~~~~~~~~~~58

Hearth Loaf ~~~~~~~~~~~~~~~~30
Herb Garden Bread ~~~~~~~~~~~56

Herbed Potato-Cheese Bread ~~~52
Irish Freckle Bread ~~~~~~~~~~~~11
Italian Loaf Rustica ~~~~~~~~~~22

Kalach ~~~~~~~~~~~~~~~~~~~~24

Liberty Bread ~~~~~~~~~~~~~~~29
Lemon Sesame Leaf ~~~~~~~~~~70

Olive Bread ~~~~~~~~~~~~~~~~19

Pear-Butter Bread ~~~~~~~~~~~~66
Pear-Hazelnut Muffins ~~~~~~~~80
Pepper Rolls ~~~~~~~~~~~~~~~~44
Peppered Squash Bread ~~~~~~~~48
Pleasant Hill Squash
  Muffins ~~~~~~~~~~~~~~~~~~73

Ruthie's Perfect
  Wheat Bread ~~~~~~~~~~~~~31
Rye and Indian Bread ~~~~~~~~57
Raspberry Streusel Muffins ~~~~78

Sally Lunn ~~~~~~~~~~~~~~~~~28
Salt Risin' Bread ~~~~~~~~~~~~~27
Sourdough Bread ~~~~~~~~~~~~14
Sweet Jammies ~~~~~~~~~~~~~~77

Vermont Oatmeal Bread ~~~~~~~33

Whole-Grain Crescent Rolls ~~~46
Whole-Wheat Bread ~~~~~~~~~~38
Whole-Wheat Cottage Loaf ~~~~39
Whole-Wheat Rolls ~~~~~~~~~~39
Whole-Wheat
  Toasting Bread ~~~~~~~~~~~34

Zucchini Dinner Rolls ~~~~~~~~45

Acknowledgments

The Corn Light Bread on page 32 from *Miss Mary's Down-Home Cooking* by
Diana Dalsass. Reprinted by permission of New American Library, Inc.
Copyright © 1985 by Diana Dalsass.
The Della Robbia Wreath on page 68 from *Judith Olney on Bread* by
Judith Olney. Reprinted by permission of Crown Publishers, Inc.
Copyright © 1985 by Judith Olney.
The Irish Freckle Bread on page 11 from *Bernard Clayton's New Complete
Book of Breads* by Bernard Clayton. Reprinted by permission of Simon & Schuster, Inc.
Copyright © 1987 by Bernard Clayton.
The Italian Loaf Rustica on page 22 by Miranda Desantis from *Pillsbury
Bake-Off® Cookbook.* Reprinted by permission of Doubleday.
Copyright © 1990 by Bantam Doubleday Dell, Inc.